# SOUL
# FREEDOM

for Irvin + Elinor,
with appreciation
James M. Dunn
7/24/2000

# SOUL
# FREEDOM

## BAPTIST BATTLE CRY

GRADY C.
# COTHEN

JAMES M.
# DUNN

SMYTH&HELWYS
PUBLISHING, INCORPORATED • MACON, GEORGIA

Smyth & Helwys Publishing, Inc.
6316 Peake Road
Macon, Georgia 31210-3960
1-800-747-3016
©2000 by Smyth & Helwys Publishing
All rights reserved.
Printed in the United States of America.

Grady C. Cothen and James M. Dunn

The paper used in this publication meets the minimum requirements of
American National Standard for Information Sciences—Permanence of
Paper for Printed Library Materials.
ANSI Z39.48–1984. (alk. paper)

Library of Congress Cataloging-in-Publication Data on File

ISBN 1-57312-335-8

# TABLE OF CONTENTS

# PREFACE

GRADY C. COTHEN

Last winter, Bill and Judith Moyers and James and Marilyn Dunn were discussing the problems of society. This is the kind of people they are. Bill and James decided that the making of books should not end. They proposed James and I write one on the assaults on soul freedom in today's cultural conflicts.

Everyone knows that Dunn is a "liberal." So, I began to examine his credentials again since I have only known him for a generation. I found that he is a corn-bread eating, fried chicken loving, Bible believing Christian. In addition, James is a church going, Christ honoring, evil bashing, separation of church and state enthusiast. Moreover, he is from Texas. His liberality is evidenced by his beliefs that there should be a free church in a free state. He feels that every soul should have direct access to God, that there should be no creeds for Baptists except the Bible, that gambling is wrong (along with lying, stealing, and adultery) and that abortion should be limited to cases involving the health of the mother, incest and rape. He believes that it is wrong to use tax money to educate perfectly normal children of Muslims or Methodists in their faith.

By the standards of Fundamentalists, some of these most Baptistic and conservative opinions may be called liberal. Actually, Dunn is theologically conservative, progressive in his understanding of the Christian's duty in a hostile world, and is the favorite target of those who disagree with these old-time conservative views.

His principal claim to liberality is that he refused to make the BJCPA a political action committee of fundamentalism.

After reviewing all this I decided that if Dunn were liberal, I would be willing to cooperate with such a man, hopefully for the discussion of some crucial issues facing the country.

The book is composed of a series of essays dealing with issues much discussed these days. Each subject is chosen to deal with an issue about which there is considerable controversy. We hope the issues chosen will ignite conversation among thoughtful people. We stand in great peril of losing the cherished principles of the free exercise of religion, the freedom from political interference with faith, and the right of self determination in all matters related to religion.

The erosion of these values is evident in many local school boards, the U. S. Congress, the political parties and many religious bodies. The dogma of the Catholic Church on the use of taxes for religious purposes has gained support from leaders of the Southern Baptist Convention. The Religious Right is now represented as the voice of the Christian faith in the market place. Political forces have distorted the faith and the faith of some has distorted the political scene.

The essays herein are postulated on the traditional Baptist heritage. My perspective is from a Southern Baptist background. The principles discussed would find assent from considerable numbers of other brands of Baptists and many other Christians.

There is much discussion around the categories of thought related to these subjects, such as modern, post-modern, personalism, individualism, isolationism, antinomianism, etc. I have not felt it desirable to attempt to fit the discussions into any such scheme of things. Present categories already form too many barriers between honest persons seeking fellowship with other Christians.

James Dunn has furnished some remarkably incisive and profound insights into modern discussions of age-old problems. I have tried to furnish modern illustrations of some of these present day confrontations.

I hope you will forgive some repetition in these essays. Some incidents or ideas illustrate several points, especially in the area of creeds, priesthood, church autonomy and freedom.

Since all of us are products to a degree of our past, and since I have no idea where I got some phrases or ideas, I will now confess that I think I have borrowed a couple from others. The idea of "cocoons" of opinion about the Bible I think I borrowed from Robison James. I borrowed the idea of Baptistification and deBaptistification from Martin Marty. If you find your favorite idea or phrase here without attribution please forgive me. Your idea lives on.

My thanks to Moyers and Dunn for the idea. Always the editors deserve better than they get for the tedious work involved in getting a manuscript ready to publish. Ray Furr and Larry Chesser especially deserve kudos. In addition, my thanks to my family for their patience during this venture. Especially thanks to Bettye who sometimes needed me while I was frozen before the computer.

To my fellow Baptists everywhere, God ain't dead. Freedom and Scripture will live on. God is not finished with his work. He called his church The Body of Christ. He may pass us by, but his work will go on.

Maranatha!

# PREFACE

JAMES M. DUNN

Been there! Done that!

That colloquial expression is useful. It may have an edge of smug superiority, a sense of accomplishment. That dimension does not at all represent the spirit of Grady C. Cothen. Yet, it says it all about the career of Dr. Cothen as a Baptist leader.

He has been there; done that. He was:
• An outstanding pastor,

• The pioneering state executive of Southern Baptists in California,

• President of Oklahoma Baptist University,

• President of New Orleans Baptist Seminary,

• President of the Southern Baptist Sunday School Board the world's largest publishing house of religious materials,

• An active leader with multiple roles in the Baptist World Alliance, and

• A founding chairman of the Religious Liberty Council, the membership arm of the Baptist Joint Committee on Public Affairs.

And these are simply the most visible public manifestations of his role as a thought leader in Baptist life over the last half of the 20th century.

So, when he and I had a long talk about what makes one a Baptist I was overwhelmed afresh. This man has tremendous authority born of experience.

Grady Cothen has brought all that "Baptist" means to his role as a founder of the Cooperative Baptist Fellowship. He comes to that role, however, not politically or ideologically. Rather, he has invested his retirement years in recapturing the Baptist essence.

He and I share some urgency in focusing on soul freedom as a great gift of Baptists.

To work with this man who has learned so much from history is joy.

To share this modest effort to communicate practical theology, not awful abstractions, is challenging.

To spend time with the Cothens ("people persons") has been enriching.

Unfortunately, there are not many competent Baptists who grasp the importance of the competency of the soul before God. In other words, there are not many Baptist leaders of the Grady Cothen ilk.

Indeed, this book comes at a time when the Baptist commitment to soul freedom feeds the deep hunger of the hearts of millions of persons seeking authenticity in religion. Yet, some anti-Baptists, pseudo-Baptists, semi-Baptists, sort-of-Baptists are retreating from the liberating faith of towering Baptists like E.Y. Mullins. We all need to be reminded of the Baptist taproot: soul freedom.

Ray Furr and Larry Chesser have done the hardest work of all. They have taken our purple prose and made it more understandable and more what we really wanted to say. Kenny Byrd has also sifted through the text. Any weaknesses we own. Any wonderful writing is their doing.

# CHAPTER ONE

# SOUL FREEDOM: UNIVERSAL HUMAN RIGHT

JAMES M. DUNN

Human rights are rooted in the Bible. The great religions of the book, Christianity, Judaism, and Islam, affirm the idea that all humankind is made in the image of God. That concept is of such transcendent importance that any difference between each human fades into nothingness by comparison.

Soul freedom, all freedom, and responsibility are God's ultimate gifts to humanity. God created and endowed all people to be free moral agents. Soul freedom and individual responsibility are not invented by government, or devised by social contract. All dignity and respect afforded persons comes from the God as revealed in Scripture.

## The Biblical Theology of Human Rights

One does not need much imagination to see that a black man is more like a white man than anything else in the world. A communist is more like a capitalist than anything else in the world. Someone rich is more like someone poor than anything else in the world.

The bond of humanity transcends all other categories: animal, vegetable and mineral. A little distance, as if we could sit out on a space platform with an astronaut; a little perspective, if we could get somewhere in time and space to allow a better look at all our strivings—that's what we need.

- Each of us is so tiny compared to the universe, even the world.
- Each of us is so much more important than things, all the stuff around us.

- Each of us is so potentially dynamic, creative, capable of changing the face of the earth.
- Each of us is so dangerous, such a time bomb, capable of evil.
- Each of us is so physically worthless (reduced to chemical value) and so valuable spiritually, to others.
- Each of us is so similar. We hope. We cry. We dream. We hurt. We laugh. We bleed.

## Our Faith That Gives Us the Perspective We Need

Dorothy Sayers believed that male and female were simply adjectives qualifying the noun *human being* and the substantive governs the modifier (*Are Women Human?*). This view is consistent with the biblical teachings regarding the oneness of the human family:

We are equal in our creaturehood. "He maketh his sun to rise on the evil and the good, and sendeth rain on the just and on the unjust." (Matthew 5:45)

We are one, being made like God. (Genesis 1:26-27)

We are one in our living, and dying and depending upon God. (Romans 14:7-13)

The overriding fact about us is our oneness. It is logically, historically, and biblically from this oneness that human rights are drawn. The biblical teachings for Jews (Deuteronomy 6:4ff) and for Christians (Mark 12:29ff) rest upon the phrase, "The Lord our God is one Lord."

Being made in His likeness we should reflect His oneness. We are, in fact, one human family. G. K. Chesterton reminded us that we are all in a small boat on a stormy sea and we owe each other a terrible loyalty.

Any honest humanism, true to its roots, will humbly admit affinity with John Donne: "Any man's death diminishes me, because I am involved in mankind, and therefore never send to know for whom the bell tolls; it tolls for thee." Donne, Canon of St. Paul's Cathedral in London, drew his worldview from Scripture.

Human rights, then, are not determined by social consensus, defined by the political process, or hammered out in a secular exercise. Human rights are more than a fad, a political agenda, a current media attraction, or an object of national policy.

## Human Rights Violations are Sin

Human rights are derived from the oneness of the human family. God gives the common bond of humanity. Human rights are not bestowed by the State, merely recognized. The *Declaration of Independence* merely affirmed and acknowledged the immutable reality. As the Russian expatriate Nicholas Berdyaev says, "without God there is no man." But there is a profound entitlement program established by God and universal in scope.

This inestimable value placed upon individuals has fueled Western life and thought. The confidence that our worth and our oneness are given, derived, the doing of the very Creator and Sustainer of the universe.

To question another's priesthood is sin. To treat persons as means rather than ends in themselves is sin. To violate the sacredness of any God reflecting, God replicating human being is sin. Sin is not simply a violation of human rights against other human beings; it is a trespass against God.

The only universal thing about human rights today is their universal violation.

With genuine creativity we seem to have found an endless string of ways to deny human rights. By entertaining the possibility of "limited" nuclear war and allowing our government to continue stockpiling overkill capacities, we take a stand against the most basic of human rights: the right of humanity to exist.

By failing to deal with conservation, environmental, and population concerns, we trade away the God-given resources of future generations. God intended for us to be caretakers of the earth, not undertakers. We continue to move toward making the earth humanly uninhabitable.

By ordering our lives as constant consumers we forget those who struggle for the basic human right. In much of the world, the battle is to maintain bare life. Our talk of human rights must take into account the 40,000 children who starve to death every day.

By tolerating economic policies in this country that victimize whole segments of the population, as blacks are now being punished with racial profiling, denial of affirmative action, the pervasive presence of trigger-happy police, we deny, in fact, our lip service to human rights. This is true no matter how pure the motives or sincere the beliefs of those who set forward long-term economic re-ordering. When, in the short term, black families are being destroyed, and hope seems almost gone, it's time to re-evaluate economic policies.

## Human Rights and God as Person

Human rights, then, are rooted in the Hebrew-Christian idea of God—God as person—not as some abstraction, not as some mystic force, not as some unseen source.

All of our human rights share the taproot of God's person and the possibility of our responding to the Divine. Our personhood is in some way beyond understanding, rooted in the God of Abraham, Isaac, and Jacob, the One whom Jesus called "Father." Because we replicate even the Creator of the Universe, all liberty, all personality, even all identity flows from that relationship.

Freedom from want and freedom for worship both relate to this doctrine of the *imago Dei*. Julius K. Nyerere, when President of Tanzania, pled this point, "We say man was created in the image of God. I refuse to imagine a God who is miserable, poor, ignorant, superstitious, fearful, oppressed and wretched—which is the lot of the majority of those He created in His own image."

## Human Rights and Shalom

Our western understanding of human rights, as almost exclusively political and social, is a fragmented grasp of human rights. The moral imperative of human rights is based solidly on the biblical vision of *shalom*: a glimpse of more than simply peace, an insight into God's intended state of well-being, wholeness, justice, completion, and harmony for all God's children. Isaiah sang, "Every valley shall be exalted, and every mountain and hill shall be made low; and the crooked places shall be made straight, and the rough places plain; and the glory of the Lord shall be revealed, and all flesh shall see it together...."

Whether we share the vision in its fullness, we understand in our hearts that nothing human is alien to any of us. We are in it together.

The oneness of the human family, the oneness of the heavenly vision, makes for a oneness of human rights. This same moral foundation pleads for freedom of conscience and freedom from torture. Precisely the spark of the Divine within all of us calls out to human worth. The response is to demand the dignity of persons. We must also respect, guard and defend the high view of God's highest creation.

## Human Rights and the Gospel

Jesus' inaugural address begins with these words: "The Spirit of the Lord is upon me, because he has anointed me to preach good news to the poor." By his own definition, which should be sufficient for any of his followers, the gospel when preached must contain a passion for the poor. When the gospel is proclaimed without evident passion for the poor, it becomes an oxymoronic expression, or a contradiction of terms. The evangelist or evangelical, whose very label comes from the word for "good news" who is not committed to the wholeness of human rights, is going against the name he or she claims.

Economic freedom is an aspect of the good news in its purest form. Jubilee 2000 seeks to link soul freedom with economic freedom. Believers around the world are calling for debt forgiveness for the poorest nations. Without it we condemn millions to misery and premature death.

The very same recognition of God's intention for all his children that moves one to intense indignation at the denial of religious freedom also makes one care about the victims of mass starvation. The very same belief that we are all made in God's image moves me to act on behalf of Kosovars and to rage at the plight of starving Sudanese, victims of their own government.

Thus, we struggle to keep belief and behavior consistent. We wrestle with disparities in our theology and our politics. We keep testing motives, our understanding, and our actions.

Acceptance of this high view of human rights has some immediate and obvious implications.

It is idealistic enough to keep us busy until the end of the journey. We will never perfectly realize the political, social, economic demands of this biblically based challenge.

It is holistic enough to take in all of life: freedom of conscience; freedom to choose one's faith and to change one's faith; freedom of thought and expression; freedom of association and travel and identification with like-minded groups; freedom from hunger and repression and torture and imprisonment for one's beliefs.

It is comprehensive enough to go beyond caring only for our own. Any commitment to human rights worthy of the name will not be restricted to concern and action for one's own nation, race, class, or clan. There is a wideness in God's mercy and to the degree we are in harmony with the biblical vision we will care about all those who are treated less than humanely.

It is, then, demanding enough that all who subscribe to this strict standard will join a perpetual minority, at least as far as the eye can see. Nothing in history suggests an early victory for human rights around the world. That minority status as advocates of human rights calls for faithfulness to our goals regardless of immediate results. It calls for spiritual resources to sustain us for the long haul. It calls for grace, patience and forbearance that will deliver us from bitterness, hatred, alienation and self-pity. We are free to fail because our rightness with God is not measured by success or the bookkeeper's bottom line at the end of the quarter. We are free to fail but we are not free to fail to act.

Christians and Jews will understand each other better and work more effectively together for justice, human dignity, and peace when we see the common soil from which our striving springs. We are not ultimately committed to the American dream or any political system or any economic philosophy. We are not and cannot be dedicated to the eradication of hunger, or to racial justice or the pursuit of peace alone on a single track, not caring about other causes. We are not operating alone in our own group or with our own objectives without a kinship with all who have caught the heavenly vision. Even though it is understandable that we specialize, even though our strivings may sometimes seem at cross purposes, those of us who seek the things that make for peace, those who respect the value of every individual and want no child to go to bed hungry tonight, those who believe that "Almighty God hath created the mind free," and those of us who seek these human rights for the whole human family, must stick together.

That seems to have been the original intention: "So God created man in his own image...male and female created he them...And God saw everything that he had made, and behold, it was very good."

Imagine the soles of two bare feet turned toward you. The two big toes represent all the human big toes on the face of the earth. Tag each of them.

This graphic game is an attempt to get at a Christian doctrine of persons. The tags for toes are intended to indicate the essence of what it means to be human from a Christian perspective. One label should indicate the *contents*.

The other tag should represent the assessment that we all make automatically or deliberately of everything and everyone that we see: a value label, a *price tag*. It will answer ideally what the creature attached to the toe is worth.

The whole odd venture is designed to see what a basic, no-frills Christianity says about personhood. Much more could be said, for certain, in any adequate theological anthropology; but much less would not satisfy, even as a starting place.

This is an attempt to re-state two elements in an elementary theological base for the nature and dignity of human beings. Could the tag on one toe read, "Made in God's image"? Augustine sang "Thou hadst made us for thyself, Oh God, and our souls are restless 'til they rest in Thee." Confessions of Augustine Pascal saw a "God-shaped emptiness in the life of every person."

Somehow, in ways one cannot explain, our personhood is defined in the biblical teaching that all humankind is made in the likeness of God.

## Human Rights and Soul Freedom

Understanding human beings in that light argues for soul freedom. There is no room for any of us to lord over others, to dominate and manipulate them, because all of us are made in the similitude of God. There is a certain arrogance when one of God's creatures claims too much control over others who, after all, come from the same mold.

Whatever else the classical teaching of *imago Dei* means, it means at least that persons, made by God, can respond to their Creator. The roots of freedom are deep within the intimate personhood of God. All true freedom is in a real sense religious freedom. It is that which replicates the Divine in all of us that makes us *response able*, responsible and free.

## Individual Freedom and Individual Responsibility

Thus, when one reflects on God's gift of free moral agency, both individual freedom and individual responsibility are not to be taken lightly. These twin concepts constitute all of humankind's link with the Eternal.

Freedom and responsibility are two parts of one process. One does not want to choose between them. Like two sides of one coin, freedom and responsibility are *indissoluble*.

Because persons are made in God's image, it is a terrible thing to tamper with them. It is especially dangerous to meddle with an aspect of a kindred soul that is so like unto their Creator's power of choice.

Kant cautioned that persons are ends unto themselves and are not to be treated as means to an end. One must recognize that persons are free to choose because God programmed them that way. People are all "wired" with *their own individual deciders*. Even though many of those decisions will be bad ones, it's serious business to rob anyone of free choice. Society reserves the right to deprive individuals of their freedom only in exceptional circumstances.

Could the tag on the other toe read, "For whom Christ died"? Augustine exclaimed, "My soul thrills within me when I think that He died for me as much as if I were the only one for whom he had to die" (*Confessions of Saint Augustine*). While being made in God's image is a belief affirmed by all of the religions which share the Genesis account as part of their sacred writings (Islam, Judaism, Christianity), the estimate of human value related to the work of Christ is distinctly Christian.

Whatever else it may mean to accept the label "Christian," to voluntarily bear that name means at least to see other human beings as valuable, possessing infinite worth. The Christian scriptures teach that followers of Jesus Christ are redeemed at great cost.

This specifically Christian belief does not diminish one iota the freedom invested in every individual. In fact, to accept the New Testament message enhances (or ought to enhance) the price tag one puts on others; for if Christ died for me as much as if I were the only one for whom he had to die, then He also loved every last human being in history with the same inestimable compassion. "For God so loved the world...."

When non-Christians look at the rigid moralism, the cocksure dogmatism, the insensitive certitude of some evangelicals who would deny soul freedom, they rightly challenge their basic Christianity. An intensity of respect for others and a dedication to their highest good characterizes Christians.

Jesus himself refused to "zap" anyone into the Kingdom of God. He died rather than call ten thousand angels to coerce. He allowed those he loved to make their own mistakes. He watched sadly as one he wanted to follow him went away, when he might have compelled him to stay.

Authentic Christianity is not morbidly obsessed with Jesus' death. No, it is inflamed with a holy zeal for the dignity of persons. Genuine Christianity is fired with a passion for persons, all persons, because of the biblical assessment of their nature and worth. The cross is not an empty symbol but a reminder of the real investment in those "for whom Christ died."

"Ye shall know the truth and the truth shall make you free."

CHAPTER TWO

# AUTHORITY IN RELIGION

GRADY C. COTHEN

*The Scriptures*
*The Holy Bible was written by men divinely inspired and is the record of*
*God's revelation of Himself to man. It is a perfect treasure of divine*
*instruction. It has God for its author, salvation for its end, and truth,*
*without any mixture of error, for its matter. It reveals the principles by*
*which God judges us; and therefore is, and will remain to the end of the*
*world, the true center of Christian union, and the supreme standard by*
*which all human conduct, creeds, and religious opinions should be tried.*
*The criterion by which the Bible is to be interpreted is Jesus Christ.*

*The Baptist Faith and Message, 1963*

"All Scripture is Profitable...." 2 Timothy 3:16

Baptists have always been known as "people of the Book." Yet, the
Fundamentalists used the Bible to fragment and seize control of the Southern
Baptist Convention. Southern Baptists have never had a creed but the Bible
since its founding in 1845. Repeated efforts by some to formulate an official
document of beliefs resulted only in two "confessions of faith." The closest we
have ever come has been *The Baptist Faith and Message*, which were statements of faith developed in 1925 and 1963. *The Baptist Faith and Message*
statements are based on The New Hampshire Confession. Both editions are
clearly not creedal, but are summaries of commonly held beliefs by those

present at the convention when they were passed. The preamble to the 1963 statement said:

(2)...We do not regard them (such statements) as complete statements of our faith, having any quality of finality or infallibility. As in the past so in the future, Baptists should hold themselves free to revise their statements of faith as may seem to them wise and expedient at any time.

Two passages in the opening of the 1963 Statement became significant when the Fundamentalists began their takeover in 1979; neither passage was precise enough for the Fundamentalists that:

(4) The sole authority for faith and practice among Baptists is the Scriptures of the Old and New Testaments. Confessions are only guides in interpretations, having no authority over the conscience...Therefore, the sole authority for faith and practice among Baptists is Jesus Christ whose will is revealed in the Holy Scriptures.

Another crucial point was contained in the statement on Scripture: ...[The Bible] has God for its author, salvation for its end, and truth, without any mixture of error, for its matter....

Every seminary and denominational agency had formal statements of loyalty to Scripture and/or commitments to adhere to its teachings as the guide to their function. Frequent accusations of "liberalism" were leveled against seminary professors or the Baptist Sunday School Board. Every conflict sought solution by reference to Scripture. Eventually, the 1963 statement of faith became the theological yardstick for measuring doctrine. Repeated efforts were made—almost annually—to amend the statement to make it more binding and creedal. In 1969 all entities of the SBC were instructed to write or teach "in conformity with and not contrary to the 1963 Baptist Faith and Message."

By the beginning of the "Fundamentalist resurgence," repeated attempts were being made to legislate specific interpretations of Scripture or the faith statements about Scripture to suit the argument of the moment. Usually references to the Bible were used to shore up a point of argument or furnish the basis for further interpretation of *The Baptist Faith and Message.* These attempts met with varied success and aroused as much opposition as support before 1979.

In 1979, the Fundamentalists said their concerns were not being addressed. They wanted to formulate guidelines to control all denominational activities. The historic Baptist stance that "we have no creed but the Bible" was no longer sufficient for the Fundamentalists. When interpretations differed from theirs, the Fundamentalists cried heresy. As the argument grew more vociferous, the denominationalists were accused of liberalism and not believing the Bible. Various proposals were made in many forums to terminate the growing controversy but the Fundamentalists did not want peace. They would not rest until they had control.

The Fundamentalists discovered that the word "inerrancy" would rally the faithful around their charges of liberalism. Their message was simple. "The people who teach in our seminaries and run our denomination do not believe the Bible." This was all they needed to arouse an emotional frenzy for those who did not know the truth.

The vast majority of Baptists on both sides of the controversy probably would have accepted at least the more precise definitions of the Chicago Statement on Inerrancy. However, the Fundamentalists were not interested in resolving issues.

They were having success using "inerrancy" as the dividing line between biblical conservatism and "liberalism." The Fundamentalists had their eyes on the denomination's purse strings, which collected some $150 million a year.

The cry of inerrancy was used to support legalistic and literal interpretations of Scripture. Virtually all of the denominational agency heads were accused of liberalism because they were said not to hold the Fundamentalist view of inerrancy. Having no desire to discuss the issue, the Fundamentalist leaders often said: "We have the votes, and this is the way it is going to be."

To these people, the basic Baptist concept of the individual transacting business with God for him/herself (priesthood) and interpreting Scripture for oneself was dangerous. The accusation was repeatedly made that if this were allowed one could "believe anything."

The truth: God dignifies a person with the right to believe anything, but each person is accountable. The Bible is full of accounts of persons He allowed to believe the wrong things and their accountability to Him.

The truth: A believer, according to historic Baptist doctrine, is limited in his belief system to scriptural truth.

Isaac Backus, one of our forefathers in religious liberty, in *An Internal Call* (1754) as quoted by Frank Mauldin adds:

> It is the common privilege of God's people to have the divine Spirit given them, to seal his truth to their hearts. It is Spirit of God, and that alone that enlightens our minds to understand his word aright, and that shows men their condition and their duty, and guides his people into all truth. God

leads his people in duty by applying home his truth, by causing divine light to shine into our understanding.

If God endows one with the right to hear the Spirit's interpretation of Scripture, the person is under no obligation to obey dictates of others. Yet, a church can determine who is in believing fellowship and an association can determine its own membership. To attempt to circumscribe the conscience of the individual by another's idea of what is acceptable theologically is to declare oneself a non-Baptist.

It was many years after the take-over of the SBC before these problems were examined with scholarly care and the involved issues clearly laid out.

It may be helpful at this point to look at the differences between the English Particular and General Baptists since it appears that various attributions of intent or content sound familiar.

Frank Louis Mauldin, in his new work *The Classic Baptist Heritage of Personal Truth*, comments on these Baptist forbears. He says that:

> [The General Baptists] think of the believer as an isolated center of experience (as a perceiver), rather than a person constituted by internal relationships with the Living God, Jesus Christ, and the beloved community....General Baptists...embrace a liberty suited to the individual subject set apart from other subjects, equally isolated and independent."

Of these Mauldin says:

> In the classic Baptist understanding of liberty, the center of reality, and thus of truth, is persons in relation, not the individual subject isolated from other subjects.
>
> Of the Particular Baptists, in the first half of the eighteenth century, who seek to 'defend God and truth' by a quest for certainty, cast a systematic theology, for they think that the man without a system {is} little more than a skeptic.' If certain knowledge is obtainable, they assert, it must begin with an axiom from which other statements in the system of belief should be logically derived.

Of the Particular Baptists he says:

> In their defense of 'the cause of God and truth' they employ the devices they oppose. First, they secure the axiom of God's sovereignty by means of argument, an all-too human agenda and a substantial portion of the dust of Zion. Second, they define sovereignty in terms of the time-bound system of hyper-Calvinistic theology. Third, their rational starting-point deflects them

away from the classic heritage which they seek to protect from the ravages of modern rationalism.

The age of Calvinistic scholasticism thus begins...and a strict orthodoxy of a decidedly rationalistic bent becomes the 'cardinal virtue of the churches'. Theological narrowness, spiritual aridity, abstruse debate and rigid creedal-ism, replace the zeal for the gospel so evident among earlier Particular Baptists....

While it appears to this writer that neither of the present day Southern Baptist groups (and those in between) are as deep into the "dust of Zion" as our predecessors, there is a remarkable parallel to present day discussions.

A clearer enunciation of the nature of the fundamentalist demands was laid out by Albert Mohler, president of The Southern Baptist Theological Seminary, in a chapter in *Beyond the Impasse* edited by Robison James and David Docker. (Nashville: Broadman Press, 1992). Mohler's belief of doctrinal adherence goes beyond the Bible. His contention is that the present conflict requires "greater clarity" than that afforded by *The Baptist Faith and Message*. While he acknowledges that the text and not the interpreter should be authoritative, "parameters must be developed" that limit the extent of beliefs. There must be "a growing shift from what can be assumed to what must be articulated."

Mohler correctly asserts that the traditionalist leaders deny any level of authority to confessional statements. However, he further asserts that there is a new consensus that demands the drawing of "articulated theological para-meters." "Southern Baptists need renewed and clearly articulated parameters as well as reaffirmation of the doctrinal center."

James Draper, former president of the SBC, joins Mohler in his position, commenting: "Proper balance within stated parameters, must be demon-strated and nurtured if our historical stance as Southern Baptists is to be preserved."

Equally disturbing to those not subscribing to these basic departures from historic Baptist principles is the overt demand that someone make a determi-nation of what is acceptable and what is not. This idea is contained in Mohler's continuation of the idea of parameters. He asserts: "A process of the-ological triage must be established in order to distinguish first-order issues on which agreement is necessary from second-order and third-order issues on which disagreement is possible."

Herein is involved many questions. Who is to do the triage? By what authority? What are the criteria for a triage? Accountable to whom? What of dissent over which order is first or third class? What is the appropriate vision of Scripture in determining the outcome of the triage?

This entire set of arguments clearly sets forth a form of propositional religion. Religious truth is to be found by interpretation of Scripture within the framework of predetermined official decisions.

Many objections can be leveled at this theological doublespeak. For example, where does an inerrant Bible fit into the triage decisions? Can conclusions arrived at by official consensus before or after consulting Scripture allow it to speak? To arrive at parameters at all is to turn toward the rationalism so criticized as belonging to the Enlightenment.

Robison James in *Beyond the Impasse*, arguing for traditional Baptist principles, stated the case succinctly. He quotes John Leland, Baptist forbear par excellence. Said Leland: "I never saw a defense of a religious system (of doctrine) but what a great part of it was designed to explain away the apparent meaning of plain texts of scripture."

Then James says:

> Neither our propositional formulation nor our objective religious experience is absolute. Both of these things are relative by being included within a 'third', namely, the mothering reality in which the first two inhere, the biblical story, the story in which the living, acting, speaking God relates to us ongoingly. (269)

James draws a conclusion that fits the discussions of today. "The trouble with the kind of system-builders whom Broadus teases and Leland lambastes, is that a lot of them are so caught up in the webs of their own systems that they cannot tell their cocoons from the Bible" (270).

The accusations that traditional Baptists have abandoned the Bible for "experience" are a tragic misrepresentation of those who disagree with the ultra-conservative movement. A careful reading of history will reveal that the present position of most of the "moderates" is more Baptistic than the creedalism of the Fundamentalists.

The issue basically devolves to the question: Do we derive our faith from the Bible and the Spirit's interpretation or do we derive it from external sources who are confident they know the mind of God by a process of triage or their interpretation of the Scripture?

For Baptists, particularly Southern Baptists, the "parameters" have always been Bible parameters determined by the conscience of the individual ideally under the leading of the Holy Spirit. This in no sense proscribes accountability. Any triage of biblical truth is prescriptive and a true Baptist asks, who prescribes?

Of course, this is not to say that there has not been a group of basic theological positions to which most Baptists subscribe. It is to say that they have been in the main clear biblical truths about which there is little controversy among conservative Christians. Any Baptist is free to subscribe or not subscribe according to his understanding of scripture.

Concerning Mohler's proposals about clarity and precision in theological matters, Molly Marshall in the same volume comments as follows:

> There is a marked inattention to religious liberty and the priesthood of all believers in his proposal, which appears to be a narrowing commensurate with the fundamental-conservative political and theological agenda. Most problematic is his call for official understanding of the nature of Scripture, something Baptists have always staunchly resisted. When one party determines how language can be employed (i.e. the meaning of "inerrancy"), a consensus can hardly emerge. (175)

The issue then again is: What is authority for a Baptist?

Contained in the arguments noted above is a clear push toward the "authority of the elite." Some person or persons must devise the parameters, perform the triage process, and make the application to the affairs of the denomination and churches.

Clearly the largest Baptist body in the world is moving away from sole dependence on Scripture for guidance—a Scripture that is claimed to be inerrant. Authority on "peripheral" matters is centered on what is in essence a creedal position.

These regulations are interpretations created by the few in power who control the functions of the denomination. Scripture viewed through the preconceptions of this minority is easily distorted to support the agenda of the elite.

Such practices move the body toward the disfranchisement of the laity, the church, and the priest.

Many of the decisions related to denominational matters are external to the Bible but governed by theological decisions theoretically based on the Bible.

Once again, where rests authority? Is it inherent in words about the Bible? Where and by whom are such pronouncements formulated? Who dictates that these are the doctrinal "parameters"? How scriptural are exclusions from fellowship based on these parameters?

Words about the Bible now control many of the functions of the denomination. An illustration is the declaration by the president of Southern Baptist Theological Seminary that he is and his forbears were "five point Calvinists." Some faculty, trustees, and a host of Baptists immediately disagreed with his view of Scripture and the straight jacket his avowal imposed.

There are many illustrations that indicate a fundamentalist mindset bound by a straight jacket of presuppositions when it comes to the Bible. All Scripture is seen through a prism (which separates light into colors) of human formulation for the understanding of the Bible. The variegated coloration of various interpretations that have evolved gives serious pause as to whether this is indeed a Baptist understanding.

The modern day arguments about Scripture sometimes sound like they are more about inherent rationalism than revelation.

With a theology of rules with endless definitions of acceptable theology, some modern so-called Baptists have arrived at a propositional formulation about the Bible instead of a primarily biblically based faith.

It is usually assumed that all persons approach Scripture with preconceived ideas. For Baptists, this predisposition is usually a simple notion that "the Bible is the inspired Word of God." Now there is a jungle of questions to be negotiated before arriving at conclusions about biblical faith. Not yet given its proper consideration is the matter of the nature of inspiration. This monumental question will someday shake the foundations of today's discussions.

The point that must not be missed is that the priest is limited by what is in Scripture, and not by the official definitions, established parameters or the predetermined interpretations that fit someone's agenda.

In the practices of the twentieth century, the creedal vision of the Bible allows much of the Bible to be ignored. The frantic insistence on forcing Christian conduct to conform to incomplete or highly selective interpretations of Scripture has left many wondering who wrote it. Continuing to disregard the central message of the Bible while fashioning a theology based on secondary issues confuses the unbeliever and misrepresents the God of the Bible.

If some without subscribing to the official interpretations can "believe anything," many within the inner sanctum of officialdom can "do anything." The strident condemnation of the moderate segment of the Baptist community has tended to obscure conduct toward them that is anything but biblical.

An important new understanding of the controversy about the Bible is now being promulgated. The claim is being made in official denominational publications that the present direction of the denomination is the proper and biblical continuance of the Baptist heritage grounded in the Reformation.

Stan Norman, theology professor at New Orleans Baptist Theological seminary, recently published an interesting discussion of the differences today in Baptist life. Norman wrote:

> Some Southern Baptists stipulate that the core, or primary Baptist distinctive is the authority of the Bible for all matters of faith and practice. Other Southern Baptists argue that Christian experience is the core Baptist distinctive. These distinctions are very real and have been with Southern Baptists for most of this century.
>
> These differences exist because of how a 'core' distinctive impacts the development of theological identity. Works on Baptist distinctives that affirm the primacy of biblical authority as the core distinctive will develop and interpret the other distinctives in light of this core. This method reflects the Protestant Reformation tradition. [Writers] believed that the Baptists and their distinctive theology were the logical outcome to the Reformation assumption of the preeminence of biblical authority. Those distinctive works that affirm the primacy of biblical authority can be categorized as 'Reformation Baptist distinctives'. Writings on Baptist distinctives that affirm Christian experience as the core distinctive embrace the Enlightenment assumption of individual autonomy. (*SBC Life*, April 1999)

Indeed it seems true that modern fundamentalism is embracing a lot of the Protestant Reformation traditions. Whether these traditions are biblical is the Baptist question. The dictations and persecutions of Protestant beginnings were neither biblical nor Baptistic.

To understand Norman's premise it is necessary to quote again:

> The Reformation tradition first asserts the primacy of biblical authority. These works construct a Baptist doctrine of the church based on biblical authority. Christian experience in its various expressions is a necessary by-product of having a New Testament church built upon biblical revelation.

Norman asserts that E. Y. Mullins was responsible for the following observation:

> The distinctive tradition moved from a core distinctive of biblical authority that shaped church life and Christian experience interpretation, to a Christian experience core distinctive that shaped biblical authority and church life...The Bible became a repository of information for individual spiritual blessings, individual Christian living, and individual freedom, rather than an authoritative revelation for a community of born-again

believers working together for the extension of God's kingdom. Christian experience replaced biblical authority as the core distinctive that interpreted the other Baptist distinctives.

Norman's basic point seems to be that the conservative part of the denomination is on course with the historic Reformation tradition—biblical authority. Moderates are "those who are more comfortable with some form of Christian experience as the foundational distinctive, tend to represent the Enlightenment distinctive tradition."

He adds the foot note:

> The category of 'Christian experience' would include those writings on Baptist distinctives, which define experiential concepts in categories such as soul competency, religious freedom, individual autonomy, the lordship of Christ, and the experience of believers baptism, to list but a few.

The Lordship of Christ not from the biblical tradition?

This arbitrary categorizing of the two groups seems to ignore several other points of view. For example, nearly all of the Baptists I have known and observed over a period of half a century were firm believers in the finality of biblical authority. Very few have been disciples of the "Christian experience" theory cited by Norman. He asserts that the "moderates" fall into the experience category and either do not accept biblical authority or have modified it to suit radical individualism. This is a fundamentalist conclusion not based on fact. This view is not born out in Mullins' writings or most other Baptist literature of the last century.

The thrust of his article seems to support the above-mentioned shift of the conservative cause toward the authority of preconceived ideas about Scripture. The authority of the church as against the freedom of the individual is a prominent theme not only in the article cited but also in many of the decisions made by the denomination. These tendencies also push decision-making upward beyond the believer or the local body of believers to the rapidly growing hierarchical structures. One cannot but wonder if we are seeing the subtle birth of "The Baptist Church", an idea resisted by Baptists for centuries.

In any case, the moderate cause is seriously miscast by Norman's arbitrary conclusions. While there has certainly been some literature representing the understanding of individualism that Norman postulates, it does not represent the majority of those now labeled "moderate." Their position does pay more attention to autonomy, rights, priesthood, and soul freedom than the so-called "Reformation" formulation. Most moderates would claim belief in biblical authority and the Axioms of Religion so carefully articulated by Mullins.

So the question of biblical authority continues to be a bone of contention within the broader fellowship of Baptists. Both sides claim its validity. Both claim to practice this doctrine in their pursuit of Christian service. The modern attempts to cloak the controversy in fine-spun definitions and critical analyses are not serving the cause of Christ. The continuing personal and group attacks on the moderates because of their refusal to submit to creedalism continue to disillusion an unbelieving public. Churches are changing their names to eliminate the word Baptist and are increasingly embarrassed to be called Baptists because of the continuing controversy.

For most of us who are called moderate, the Bible remains the sole rule of faith and practice. We also believe that it supports and teaches soul competency (certainly not church competency over the soul), religious freedom (upon which the country was founded), individual autonomy, (Christ related to individuals making them responsible for themselves), the lordship of Christ (what other Lord is there?) and believer's baptism for the protection of a regenerate membership. The church is the bride of Christ.

The Bible need not be prefaced by a list of specified conclusions. It is the word of God, inspired by him and interpreted for the priest by the Holy Spirit. No true Baptist would claim infallibility in his interpretations. Certainly the church is important and should nourish the believer and teach him/her and minister in the name of Christ. The church is the helper, teacher, minister, worship center, and missioner, not the believer's master.

While the majority of this chapter discusses the conflicts among those historically called Southern Baptists, others of our Baptist family have suffered many of the same conflicts. The doctrines of scripture and freedom are worth disagreeing about and even separating about. As various Baptist groups have struggled with these and other issues, most have sought to be held by cardinal principles that are central to being who we are.

These kinds of issues are being struggled with in many places in the earth—often using different names and points of contention. The basic problems involve whether persons are free to practice the convictions of their conscience or whether they will be controlled by a religious elite, an organized church, the state, or a state church. Untold thousands of lives have been given in these struggles and other millions have suffered the basic inability to change their plight.

The forces of authoritarianism are loose in America. They have seriously influenced the law-making bodies at every level and continue to harass those who disagree. Historically Baptists have resisted these forces, not joined them. From Helwys' word to the king of England, "Thou art the king, not God" to modern protests to the congress over church-state matters, true Baptists believe authority in religion is the Bible.

# CHAPTER THREE

# NOT BY FORCE BUT BY FAITH... ALL EVANGELISM PREDICATED UPON SOUL FREEDOM

### JAMES M. DUNN

All authentic missions and evangelism are predicated upon the possibility, the opportunity, and the responsibility of a voluntary response. We call it *soul freedom*.

The zeal of Baptist evangelists has left the impression that even the most responsible Baptist preachers would "compel them to come into the Kingdom of God" at all costs.

The most enthusiastic used car dealer has nothing on many Baptist evangelists moving in for the kill. To attend a Baptist convention or pastors' conference and pay attention to the fulsome fixation on statistics would reinforce that popular impression.

This much should be clear. I, personally, am a born-again, Texas-bred, Spirit-led, corn bread-fed Baptist. I still preach "revivals" though most churches "east of the River" and north of the Mason-Dixon are too sophisticated to call them that—they are "preaching missions."

I invite folks to accept Jesus Christ as personal Savior. I believe people need the Lord. I am not ashamed of the Good News, and I proclaim it on my own time without government supervision. Can you imagine an altar call, a revivalistic invitation, being extended to a captive audience of 6- to 12-year-olds in a public school setting? It happens.

According to the *Charleston* (WV) *Gazette* in January, 1998 (not colonial America) Andy Waddell of Maysel wrote to two Clay County elementary school principals protesting Christmas programs that included prayers and altar calls, where people can publicly proclaim they have been saved.

Principal John Gency, a local preacher, made the altar call at Clay Elementary. According to Waddell, Gency said, "If you don't know Jesus Christ as your personal Savior, come forth now...witness and be saved."

Sensitivity to soul freedom marks mature missions. An eagerness to respect each individual characterizes responsible evangelism.

Some serious responsibility to respect the integrity of other individuals is an essential corollary of practicing soul freedom. To claim the rights and privileges of responding for one's own soul absolutely demands that one afford the same opportunity to others.

I shudder to think of all the young lives that have been damaged forever by attempts to force a decision for Christianity upon those who were yet too young to understand. Could it be that as the pioneer Christian educator, J. M. Price, said, "We are as responsible for those people whose experiences we bungle as we are for those we never reach at all"? Makes sense to me. I grew up in a church where once a year a preacher, usually a visiting evangelist, was presented to the 6- to 12-year-old children. He would make an over-simple, over-emotional, often fear-inducing, appeal to all the boys and girls to trust Jesus or go to hell. Kathleen Norris, in her great book *Amazing Grace*, catches the spirit of such appeals. She says the message of "revival-style theology" is "only believe that God loves you or he'll send you to hell forever."

We came to call such urgent child evangelism "trap services." Kids more or less innocently attending Sunday school found themselves objects of high-pressure super salesmen. High-pressure tactics, manipulation, and other such spiritual child abuses trample the spirit of soul freedom.

The many threats to soul freedom and authentic evangelism are clear. One is triumphalism. This spirit is not academic. I speak from experience. I grew up in a Baptist church where we were taught to be soul winners. To be a witness to the power of God was not enough. To share our faith lovingly and to depend upon the Holy Spirit to convict of sin and righteousness was not adequate. We had to "draw the net" and we were taught how to do just that. Many, if not most, conservative Christians today have a better understanding of evangelism, but militant, manipulative "outreach programs" are alive and well.

Sometimes the triumphalism is so theologically parochial, so evangelistically fueled, and so ethically insensitive that outsiders cannot even imagine its depth and pervasiveness. An excellent illustration is the current attempt to comprehend the anti-Semitism of pro-Israel evangelicals. Of course, it's possible, maybe even necessary, to tout the nation Israel without loving Jews, caring about religious freedom or respecting their history or beliefs. One may merely observe the Southern Baptist campaign "targeting" Jews. For take-over-minded fundamentalists, Jews are but pawns for a narrow Armageddon eschatology and/or prospects for evangelism—hardly candidates for an "I-Thou" relationship.

There's no such thing as real evangelism without real religious freedom. Real evangelism admits from the outset the sanctity of free choice.

Every invitation to accept Christ, every proclamation of the good news, every missionary impulse springs from the belief that those who hear the gospel are able to respond to it. The evangelistic assumption is that the human subjects, the personal targets, the individual recipients of the truth, if you will, may accept or reject the message as it is presented.

One secret of the immense popularity of the Baptist version of the Faith lies in twin presuppositions: (1) the urgency of sharing the love of Jesus Christ with a lost and dying world, and (2) the possibility that any human being touched by God's grace will genuinely be transformed by the saving power of Jesus Christ.

Baptists at our best have been characterized as passionately evangelistic and compassionately missionary. We are eager witnesses to the truth, as we know the truth must be told. We share our personal faith unashamedly, not to run up the tally of believers or put notches on our gospel gun, but because we must. We tell others about our religious experiences because we think it is worth telling. As D. T. Niles said, the spread of Christianity depends upon "one beggar telling another where to find a crust of bread." All Baptist Christians may not be able to articulate a theology of evangelism, but the word is spread by them "doing what comes naturally."

Baptists have also insisted upon respect for the individual. We have rejected coercion in matters spiritual. We do not approve of trickery and manipulation to gain agreement with our views. Threats, cheap appeals to fear and hate, bandwagon born-againism, sinful over-simplification, and hard-sell tactics are off limits for those who understand the intimate, inner nature of one's Christian beginnings.

We know that one accepts Jesus Christ as Savior freely or not really at all. Voluntary religion, in Baptist eyes, is the only valid religion. All believers are not able to spell out a doctrine of free moral agency, but they understand it in their innards. And so, the slogan "soul freedom" has gained great currency.

When Jesus dealt with the rich young ruler (Matt. 19), he set out the terms of discipleship. Christ told the inquirer in plain language what it would take to be one of his followers.

One cannot imagine a disinterested Jesus. The master teacher cared deeply about his student. The Rabbi was meaningfully engaged with his would-be follower. Yet, the young man went away "very sad," "sorrowful."

Jesus did not trip him, zap him, call him back, or offer some inducement for him to change his mind. Rather, the whole of Jesus' own ministry reflects his profound respect for his hearers. He refused to run roughshod over anyone or to violate conscience.

The Bible is full of evidence that God wants only volunteers in His regiment. For all the mistakes and misjudgments, with all the sin and greed, despite all the evil resulting from human free will, the Bible story makes it plain that true religion is never forced. St. Bernard wrote:

> Take away free will and there remaineth nothing to be saved....Salvation is given by God alone and it is given only to the free will even as it cannot be wrought without the consent of the receiver; it cannot be wrought without the grace of the giver.

Every "whosoever will" in the Bible reminds us of the free choice essential to authentic Christianity. Religious freedom, then, may be seen as inextricable from any evangelism worthy of the name. It is a strange development, indeed, when persons called evangelicals are callous to appeals for real religious liberty. Any proper relationship of freedom and evangelism magnifies their indissolubility. Should one have to choose between evangelism and freedom, the choice would be like having to decide between breathing out and breathing in. We'd all prefer to continue both.

Cannot zealots command faith, demand discipleship, order society to shape up spiritually? No! It simply cannot be done, because we know better. In the long haul, the losers will be those who would enforce creeds, burn books, or violate conscience for consensus' sake. The God who gave us life gave us liberty at the same time.

The Creator wired us up with freedom and responsibility all tangled. We're programmed, to use a modern verb, with responsibility that presupposes freedom and freedom that can exist only in responsibility. The incisive Dietrich Bonhoeffer came close to exposing the elusive but immutable connection between religious freedom and responsible religion in his discussion of obedience and freedom:

Obedience without freedom is slavery; freedom without obedience is arbitrary self-will.

Obedience restrains freedom; and freedom ennobles obedience.

Obedience binds the creature to the Creator, and freedom enables the creature to stand before the Creator as one who is made in His image.

Obedience shows people that they must allow themselves to be told what is good and what God requires of them (Micah 6:8); and liberty enables them to do good themselves.

Evangelism, rightly understood, is an impossible endeavor without religious freedom protected by the institutional separation of church and state. Religious freedom marks off the playing field, establishes the market place, and provides the context in which all faiths may offer their own understanding of the ultimate good news from heaven to humankind.

For freedom we are set free.

# CHAPTER FOUR

# SOUL FREEDOM AND DEBAPTISTIFICATION

GRADY C. COTHEN

*The sole authority for faith and practice among Baptists is the Scriptures of the old and New Testaments. Confessions are only guides in interpretation, having no authority over the conscience....Baptists are a people who profess a living faith. This faith is rooted and grounded in Jesus Christ who is 'the same yesterday, and today, and for ever.' Therefore, the sole authority for faith and practice among Baptists is Jesus Christ whose will is revealed in the Holy Scriptures.*

*Baptist Faith and Message, 1963*

"...Truth shall make you free." John 8:32

The Baptist mystique that separates this group from other Christians in matters of polity and governance is rooted in the idea of the priesthood of all believers, autonomy and democracy of every entity at every level of the denomination. Baptists believe that every believer is capable of transacting business with God for him/herself. There is no necessity for a translator of God's message though teaching, nurture, and worship have their places. There is no official repository for divine truth or instruction save the Bible interpreted to the individual by the Holy Spirit.

Each person has equal rights in the church. And the church is thus democratic and each church is independent. Involved also is the idea that only the local church can ordain a minister and, while outsiders are often invited to participate in the examination and ordination, the decision rests with the local church. The same rationale exists for the placing of ministers. Only the local body can make such a determination, and its decision is final. The local body has entire control of its finances and contributions to the cooperating bodies, determination of its own membership, and any other matters relating to its direction and welfare. This freewheeling ecclesiology has produced some remarkable results.

Baptists in the schemes of other Christians have been neither fish nor foul. Baptists have been denied designation as a "mainstream denomination" because of various differences in perspective and emphasis. Baptists often have seen themselves as different from other evangelicals for a variety of reasons, including a sometimes-extreme emphasis on denominationalism.

Across the years, there has been a distinct Baptist tradition that has been featured in Southern Baptist denominationalism. The tradition has been a combination of beliefs and practices that have distinguished the group from other evangelicals. Some of these apply to other Baptists groups, too.

In summary, features combine to produce an almost unique religious body:

(1) All Southern Baptist entities from the individual priest to the local church to the local association of churches to the state or district conventions to the national convention have been free, independent, and autonomous. Each unit has right of self-determination and is democratic in its decision-making. Each relates to others by choice according to its understanding of God's leadership. Each body determines its own membership.

These ideas are not recent or newly conceived in this generation. Thomas Henderson Pritchard, a president of Wake Forest College who died more than 100 years ago (d. 1896), wrote in 1888:

As to church government, we believe that each separate and individual church is entirely independent of all other churches, persona, and bodies of men either civic or ecclesiastical, and is to be governed by its own members alone, without aid or interference of any other person or persons whatever. (*Biblical Recorder*, June 1998)

Here was a system based on free exercise of religion, vis-à-vis government and other religious bodies:

(2) Voluntary cooperation within the bodies, on different levels of function, for common good. Relationships between local, state or district and national bodies sustained on a voluntary basis.

(3) Institutions have been governed by the founding bodies through delegated authority, existing independently, and within a loose framework of collegial agreements.

(4) These institutions responsible through trustees elected for fixed terms have usually operated with due regard to the opinions of dissent and criticism.

(5) The sponsoring bodies and the trustees brooked no interference in governance from outside interests.

(6) The independent units related to the others fraternally and were often mutually supportive.

(7) In the denomination on the local, state, and national levels, there was no centralized authority. These bodies exercised limited authority over their institutions except through trustees elected for fixed terms.

It appears that some of these verbs need to be past tense now in light of many changes described below.

Behind all this has been unorganized and largely uncontrolled political activity. Before 1979, when an organized group emerged with the avowed purpose of controlling the denomination, each annual meeting of the various bodies brought its own milieu or set of issues often resolved on the spot. There was little organized effort to control the affairs of the various units.

The impossible disorganized set of entities mentioned above produced a remarkable and very effective array of institutions and service agencies.

The states produced more than half a hundred colleges and universities ranging in effectiveness from just adequate to superior. Childcare facilities, hospitals, conference centers, and church service facilities and personnel were provided in the states desiring them. The national body produced six seminaries, national and international mission-sending agencies, the nation's largest religious publishing house, and commissions sponsoring a variety of interests from preservation of historical materials to radio and television services.

Pastors, ordinary people, professors, writers, speakers, and organizations influenced this multitude of agencies. They were ultimately controlled by Baptists en masse interested in their welfare through a board of trustees.

It was difficult to keep this organized confusion from becoming disorganized chaos. This suited Baptists because it meant that there were no little democrats behind the scenes controlling the democracy. To be sure, there were leaders in each phase of the work but each was limited to his sphere of service, obligated to his organization by a constitution and bylaws and subject to constant scrutiny by anyone who wanted to inquire. Some had considerable influence in a larger body but little authority beyond the organization they led. Often someone else wanted the positions of leadership and sometimes succeeded, but only with the vote and support of the majority. The majority was a following people who were willing to let someone else lead so long as the direction was acceptable.

Technically on the national level, the president of the Southern Baptist Convention appointed a committee on committees, which nominated the committee on boards, which nominated the members of the boards of directors of the agencies. These then were elected by the national convention in its annual meeting. Whatever imbalance occurred could be corrected at the next meeting. For more than a 100 years, some variation of the system functioned quite well.

As the Cultural Revolution swept America, the SBC was radically changed. For a number of years several people felt left out of the leadership circle. These were usually people who invested little of themselves, their churches, or their money in the denomination. A number of controversies arose during the 1960s and 1970s over a variety of matters. The charges of "liberalism" were made against the seminaries, the Sunday School Board and some leaders.

By 1979, Paul Pressler, a Texas judge with a Presbyterian background, discovered how to seize control of the vast denominational machinery. He had been imagining liberals everywhere since his days at Princeton. He allied himself with Paige Patterson, a young theologian who thought he had found liberals in his seminary faculty. One version has it that the young man's father, a Texas Baptist executive director, had patted him on the head and announced that this boy would save the convention from the liberals. Whatever the truth of that statement, he felt it was his calling to do so. Pressler and Patterson set out to take over the denomination. By 1979, they had enough votes to elect a president of the SBC whose appointments to the committee on committees "were just perfect." This meant that they would place people on the committee on nominations that would control the election of trustees to the agencies. The reaction of those leading the denomination was mingled fear and ignorance. They were fragmented and ineffective.

By 1985, the process had gained control of all the agencies and institutions of the national convention for the Fundamentalists. The details of these events are adequately reported elsewhere.

Radical changes took place in the old denomination. Nominations for the boards of directors of the seminaries, publishing house, commissions, and especially the Executive Committee were made only from "those who were with us in the struggle". Early on in the conflict, the Fundamentalists said they only wanted "parity" on the boards—meaning a balance of conservatives and moderates. The Fundamentalists lied about parity. They wanted complete control to purge the whole system so that it was loyal to a few men. When they had enough votes in the national body, all nominees were from the Fundamentalist bloc as they are today.

Curiously, the way to complete control of all functions was along the path that the Fundamentalists had criticized the former leadership for following.

When the moderates became aware of the implications of the process of trustee selection, an attempt was made on a number of occasions to amend the report of the Committee on Nominations. Finally, the Fundamentalist majority passed the following crippling change: "...The motion may be amended but no messenger shall be allowed to propose more than one (1) person at a time for election..." (*SBC Annual* 1991, p. 35). In light of the hundreds of people nominated annually for the boards of the national body, this presented an impossible task for the moderates. The president sometimes conveniently lost his hearing and sight when these replacement nominations were introduced.

With the fundamentalist control, 70 or 80 pastors of the mega-churches decided the determination of the candidates for president. Each year that a new president was to be elected, the group met in a closed meeting "for prayer" and to discuss "the future." No credible press representatives or uninvited guests were permitted to attend. This method and group aroused so much interest and resentment among the traditional leadership that the shakers and movers were promptly named the "college of cardinals."

With one exception, the decisions of this group on the selection of the president have been carried out since 1979 without serious deviation. In the one exception, they fired one seminary president too many and a backlash occurred that resulted in the election of an unanointed man, though he had been accounted as one with them in the "resurgence."

The nominations for president by the "college" became so rigidly controlled that Toby Druin, editor of the Baptist Standard of Texas, suggested in an editorial that the members of the convention simply not vote on a president since the die was cast. When control of the national body was achieved, all sorts of changes began. Some were quite radical. It was decided that the national structure should be re-engineered. Without the usual careful and prolonged preparation for change, the Executive Committee appointed a committee to recommend a changed and reduced structure. For many years, the Fundamentalist faction had complained about the organization of the convention. The committee was made up of persons who had had little experience in denominational matters, with only one of them having had brief experience in heading an agency. The committee was composed of two pastors, one associate pastor, a lawyer, a "financial strategist," and the controversial president of Southern Baptist Theological Seminary. They declared that they would not allow press coverage in their deliberations. Few reports were made even to the appointing body, none of genuine significance to the whole convention.

After a prolonged study, their recommendations were presented to the Executive Committee for decision without significant input from those affected by the report. For example, one executive said that he heard on a Friday night that his organization would be recommended for abolishment on Monday. Several agency heads later said that they had had no significant opportunity to contribute to the deliberations about their organizations. Their trustees were not consulted except by letter.

Despite the lengthy study, which completely changed the functions of the national body, the plan was presented to the parent committee on Monday evening, February 20, 1993 for vote on the following day. The vote to recommend to the convention was 64 to 3 in favor of adoption. No one outside the inner circle had an opportunity to adequately study or comment on the completed recommendation.

The convention affirmed the overhaul overwhelmingly and repeated it the following year to satisfy constitutional requirements. The recommendations were far-reaching and included:

(1) Reduce the number or SBC agencies from 19 to 12.
(2) Eliminate the Commissions including Education, Stewardship, Historical, Brotherhood, Radio and Television and the Commission on the American Baptist Theological Seminary.
(3) Consolidate the Brotherhood Commission and Radio and Television Commission with the Home Mission Board to become the North American Mission Board.
(4) Remove from Woman's Missionary Union the SBC assignments to develop women's ministries and raise money for the two mission boards. Assign the money raising responsibilities to the mission boards.
(5) Assign to the Sunday School Board responsibility to supervise ministries for laypersons, stewardship education, and capital fund raising; and assist churches with Christian schools and home-schooling ministries.

(6) Limit the services of the Annuity Board to serving church employees qualified by state conventions, employees of qualified Baptist associations, employees of state convention and their subsidiaries, and employees of the entities of the SBC and their subsidiaries.

In addition, the first-term trustees of the new North American Mission Board were dismissed and the reorganization committee named the new ones. One member of the committee involved in these far-reaching changes accepted the presidency of the mission board and another became a top associate.

These changes were touted as providing for great savings to be used for the mission boards and seminaries. No substantive detailed report has ever been made public proving these assertions. To this point any additional money has gone to the Executive Committee, the Ethics Commission, and the seminaries.

The methods used in this upheaval overshadowed the worth of some worthwhile changes. There was remarkably little criticism of some of the changes that would ultimately wreak the most havoc. The worst was yet to come.

With little fan fare, the Executive Committee put itself in the catbird's seat by steering the reorganization. The Committee became the "sole member of the corporation" of the Baptist Foundation. This move solidified the Committee's control of the body that handled large sums of the denomination and depositor's funds. The number of trustees was immediately reduced from more than 30 to 7, chosen by the Executive Committee. The president of the Executive Committee was made chairman of the board and a member of the administrative and investment committees of the Foundation.

The press reported that the President of the Executive Committee also was made a member of the President's Council of Seminary Presidents. Since its organization, this body was constituted only of the presidents who agreed that all decisions concerning the budget formula must be unanimous. If this provision remains intact, and it is very likely that it will, the President of the Executive Committee will have serious influence if not final control of those deliberations. Including itself, the Executive Committee now has control or serious power in eight of the twelve remaining agencies and practical budgetary control over three others.

A long series of deliberations has ensued over the Executive Committee's desire to direct the affairs of the Annuity Board. To one outside the sphere of Baptist life, all this may seem ordinary. Several things about it are extraordinary. Such radical change in structure and function had never occurred. Such changes as had been made were long planned, widely publicized and publicly discussed.

Most serious is the concentration of power within the Executive Committee, which has been carefully avoided for many years. Since the "college of cardinals" either seized the power of nomination or was allowed to assume the right of nomination of the coming president of the national body, the convention has had little meaningful debate about anything. The word is abroad that one is in cooperation or isolation, take your choice.

Previously one of the overriding principles of the operation of the convention's business had been openness that created trust. Certainly much talk of any change or decision occurred in small informal groups. When official bodies met, the deliberations were usually open. In forty years of service in the denomination I can remember maybe a half-dozen closed sessions. These usually had to do with personnel decisions or matters related to legal problems.

Executive sessions during the transition in the convention were common. The Sunday School Board, The Foreign Mission Board, The Home Mission Board, the Executive Committee, the seminary trustees, and the commissions all had their times of closed deliberations. Southern Baptist Seminary, in its spate of firings, resignations, debate, and turmoil, probably led the way in the number of closed sessions. Shortly after its birth the International Mission Board announced that it would regularly at each meeting of the trustees hold a closed meeting to discuss its business.

Even before the reorganization accentuated the changes, the president of the then Foreign Mission Board, Keith Parks, offered his resignation. He told the ABP "a few of the changes I see." He listed:

- Ultra-conservative theological interpretations, not mission principles, are driving trustee decisions.
- Suspicion, distrust, criticism, and intimidation have replaced trust and respect for differences.
- Freedom to disagree has been replaced by expectation of conformity.
- Prospective staff members are asked to express loyalty to the trustees or the SBC 'conservative resurgence.'
- Prospective missionaries are asked to affirm the four examples of biblical inerrancy cited in the SBC Peace Committee report.

Parks added:
I feel we are missing the best that God had for us. Southern Baptists should be marching through God's door of opportunity as a united, loving, obedient people of God. May God forgive us and have mercy on us.

A recent example of such a radical change in mission policy has caused widespread confusion and anger. The Board historically functioned with the missionaries in a given mission—such as Nigeria—making the decisions about the business of that mission. They formulated the budget, decided on the priorities for the coming year, made certain decisions on missionary personnel, and saw to other matters related to that area. This was an important part of the mission's work and annually a week or so was set aside for these significant gatherings. With the new regime, the missionaries were told that they no longer had these functions. An administrative team appointed in Richmond would make these decisions. Obviously, the missionaries were disturbed by these changes and exclusion from decisions relating to their work. Several couples returning to America reported that they were told in effect, "Accept it or catch the next plane home."

These citations mean that often-controversial matters are dealt with behind closed doors, opposing opinions seldom see the light of public discussion, dominant personalities control certain issues with no public exposure, and policy matters are settled without public participation.

Power and authority once again have been concentrated in unBaptistic ways.

Concerning decision-making in private meetings, some of the results have been astounding. The termination of many long-time employees has been accomplished privately without due process. The heads of most of the deleted agencies had their fate sealed before the reorganization committee reported to the Executive Committee. For a long list of the terminated and their trials, or rather lack thereof, see the section "The Slaughter of the Innocents" in Chapter 12.

While these kinds of proceedings are common in many other institutions, they have been minimal among Southern Baptists in the past. While open deliberations are often painful and sometimes embarrassing, they are essential to trust and cooperation. It is at the point of loss of trust that the denomination has suffered its greatest tragedy.

Another radical change in SBC operations related to the affiliated churches. Many in the SBC vocal leadership felt that certain kinds of conduct were unacceptable in the churches affiliated with the SBC. This was beyond any concept previously held by the convention. Previously the only qualification for affiliation with the SBC was financial gifts by churches in "friendly cooperation" with the convention. Now it was deemed essential to pass a constitutional provision: "Among churches not in cooperation with the Convention are churches that affirm, approve of, or endorse homosexual behavior" (*SBC Constitution, Article III, Section 1*). One or two churches that either accepted known homosexuals or ordained them as pastor or deacon prompted this. Grievous questions abound about whether other sins will be or should be dealt with in the future. This reminds me of a J. D. Grey story. When Grey was president of the convention, he said to his church, "Where would we be if all liars suddenly disappeared? I would be up here preaching to empty pews!"

Immediately some state conventions began the process of setting up guidelines to control the churches affiliated with their organization.

The Florida convention defined some criteria by which a church would be measured for membership. Previously the requirements for affiliation were contribution of $250 to the convention's work and friendly cooperation with the body. In 1996, the convention was asked to establish a new set of criteria that would "examine theology, faith, practice and polity". The state Board would assign the task to a committee and "approve any guidelines and procedures to be followed by the Board."

This unprecedented move for a Southern Baptist body added the requirement that any church not a member of a local association of churches of specified size must subscribe to a statement of faith that agrees with *The Baptist Faith and Message*.

In Oklahoma, a similar kind of problem was brewing. The change proposed said in part: "Cooperation shall be evidenced by fellowship and cooperation with an association of Southern Baptist churches, and the Baptist General Convention of Oklahoma." Further: "It will be the responsibility of the association to notify the executive director-treasurer in the event an affiliate ceases to cooperate." Baptists have historically refused to place in the hands of one entity control over another's membership. Here a director of missions is in the precarious position of being able to lead an association to blackball a church for affiliation with the state convention.

In Georgia, the convention considered an amendment to the constitution to put in place a process for withdrawing fellowship from member churches that "1) affirm, approve or endorse homosexual behavior or 2) engage in non-biblical charismatic worship practices that are divisive and disruptive." (*BP*, November 1988) The section on homosexuality passed by a large vote but the section on charismatic practices failed to meet the two-thirds vote needed to change the constitution.

Two points should be made on these movements. Baptists historically have left matters of doctrine that absolutely required some action to protect the integrity of the larger body to local associations. Second, the passage of some restrictions based on scriptural passages opens the door to the logical consideration of all such violations. While homosexuality is generally believed to be contrary to scripture, what of the more generally pervasive problems of adultery, fornication, hatred, greed, and an infinite number of other biblically proscribed acts? Previously Baptists have thought that these decisions are not in the purview of the denominational bodies.

Our American Baptist brothers and sisters are having their share of conflict over such issues. Though their polity differs from the SBC, their concept of the autonomy of the local church is in jeopardy. The American Baptist Churches, U. S. A. General Board voted to expel four churches from the denomination over their "welcoming and affirming" stance toward homosexuals. The vote of the Board to expel in one case was 77-76, in another 83-70, another 83-71, and in the fourth 82-72. Some Board members said the vote might lead to a major rift in the 1.5 member convention. Daniel Weiss, General Secretary, raised the logical question as to what other sins would be raised as barriers to fellowship. Whatever else may be said, it is certain that deBaptistification is alive beyond the Southern clan.

To demonstrate the surge of non-Baptist ecclesiology, a motion was made at the SBC national meeting to rebuke the Immanuel Baptist Church of Little Rock for the conduct of its most famous member, the President of the United States. This was at least the second such attempt. Fortunately more Baptistic heads prevailed with considerable criticism from the less Baptistic critics.

The local church, which traditionally was immune to the perambulation of the larger bodies thus, has come in for its share of actions directed at its conduct and decisions. The democracy and independence of the local body traditionally was without question in spite of occasional attempts of a larger body to give instructions.

The national convention, which had been severely criticized by the more moderate minority for its actions, took a radical action related to mission giving. Traditional Baptists for fellowship and mission activities organized the Cooperative Baptist Fellowship. Originally, the funding mechanism for the group was called The Baptist Cooperative Mission Program, Inc. It was intended that the churches that did not agree with the direction of the fundamentalist leadership of the SBC could give through the new channel to the mission agencies and seminaries of the convention while omitting other causes. While such avenues of giving already existed through designations, the intent of the new method was to allow the churches to do what they wanted.

Immediately substantial sums of money began to flow to various agencies while others were omitted.

The new SBC leadership decided that no money should be accepted that was given through what became the Cooperative Baptist Fellowship. Practically, this meant that the church was directed to give in the accepted manner, or its funds would not be received. For the first time in Southern Baptist history, a church was told how it must give.

The matter grew even more serious when persons from churches that cooperated with or gave funds to the Cooperative Baptist Fellowship began to be excluded from service on a national board (and some state boards.) On several occasions, persons who attended or spoke at a national or state meeting of the Fellowship were excluded from state committees or boards.

Leaders who before the "conservative resurgence" regularly gave to and participated in non-Baptist causes of considerable variety inaugurated this flagrant violation of usual Baptist practice. Some of these persons had had considerable involvement with various para-church movements that usually had little reference to the local churches.

One of the more serious pronouncements of the national body affecting the local church came in a resolution ostensibly affirming the priesthood of the believer. A portion of the resolution, however, seemed to deliver the true purpose of the effort. It said:

> ...The doctrine of the priesthood of the believer in no way contradicts the biblical understanding of the role, responsibility, and authority of the pastor which is seen in the command to the local church in Hebrews 13:17, 'obey your leaders, and submit to them; for they keep watch over your souls, as those who will give an account;...be it finally Resolved, that we affirm the truth that elders, or pastors, are called of God to lead the local church (Acts 20:28). (*SBC Annual* 1988, p.69)

Many Greek scholars believe this is a serious mistranslation of the text cited on obedience. Lay leaders in the churches are not fond of the idea of obeying a pastor of a church.

Various public pronouncements and convention actions made it abundantly clear that the churches had no business ordaining women as deacons or ministers. Several associations followed the obvious intent of the national body by excluding churches that ordained women as deacons. Particularly objectionable was the idea of ordaining a woman as a "senior pastor." The national body added an additional article to the confessional statement concerning women that was widely interpreted as requiring women to submit to their husbands. The problematic statement says: "A wife is to submit herself graciously to the servant leadership of her husband even as the church willingly submits to the head ship of Christ."

The "Commentary" that accompanied the change in *The Baptist Faith and Message* reads in part:

> Wives on the other hand were created to be 'helpers' to their husbands (Gen. 2:18). A wife's submission to her husband does not decrease her worth but rather enhances her value to her husband and to the Lord (I Peter 3:4). This humble and voluntary yielding of a wife to her husband's leadership becomes a resource for evangelism (1 Pet.3: 1-2), an opportunity for glorifying God (1 Pet. 3:4-6), a channel for spiritual growth as ultimately the wife trusts herself to the Lord, and a means for bringing honor to His Word (Titus 2:3-5). (*SBC Annual* 1998, p.80)

After much national amusement and anger by various comedians and other commentators, many different interpretations of the statement have been published, trying to allay the criticism.

All these theological, governmental and prejudicial shenanigans led by the fundamentalist majority began to have serious effects on the churches. A considerable number of churches dropped the name "Baptist." Some new churches refused to list themselves as Baptist though professed Baptists organized them. A few churches disassociated themselves from the SBC. A considerable number discontinued their gifts to the denomination. Many churches have or are considering the reallocation of mission funds.

In this context, Michael Johnson, professor at Mississippi College, spent his sabbatical visiting 43 churches in 24 states known for their religious education programs. Twenty-two of them were Baptist. Of the 22 Baptist churches he visited, half are in the process of taking or have already taken the word "Baptist" out of their name. "They claim to be maintaining their Baptist identity, but only in that they continue to contribute to the Cooperative Program." He showed membership manuals and new member training materials of several churches. They emphasized beliefs about God, Christ, and the Bible. "They make virtually no mention of Baptist history, heritage, or Baptist principles." He further indicated that many of the churches were writing their own Sunday school materials—especially in the preschool and children's areas.

One of the most far-reaching results of the debaptistification of the SBC has been the reaction of the Baptist General Convention of Texas. Texas has more Baptists than any other state and has normally given much more money to the denomination than any other group of churches. The national leaders for not joining enthusiastically in the revolution have frequently criticized the state leadership. Texans, proud of their numbers and strength, have felt ignored, slighted, and condemned by the national body. When a recent meeting of the convention met in Texas, the Executive Director was not even invited to welcome the meeting to Texas. This was a serious matter to Texans and a gratuitous insult to the strongest constituent body.

Bill Pinson, Executive Director of the Baptist General Convention of Texas, recently highlighted some of these problems:

> When the organized political effort in the SBC began in 1979, Texas Baptists were as they had always been—committed to the Bible as their authority, theologically conservative and focused on missions and evangelism. Although in 1979 some or even many Texas Baptists may have viewed certain Southern Baptists and some SBC seminaries in the East as 'liberal', most did not favor imposing creedal views or requiring conformity of belief on theological and social issues. Thus, the call of the political leaders of the so-called 'conservative resurgence' seemed either unnecessary or dangerous to many Texas Baptists. The secular political activity, the character assassination, the exclusion from positions of leadership of any but those who were part of the cause, and the firing or forcing from office of persons who did not agree with their political agenda offended and even enraged many Texas Baptists. (Mark Wingfield, *Baptist Standard*, June 1999)

Perhaps as important has been the growing feeling of the apparent majority of Texas Baptists that the denomination has ceased to be the Southern Baptist Convention they knew and loved. Of considerable concern are many of the matters mentioned above and a general feeling that Baptistic principles have been forfeited to the search for power and control. Texas Baptists reacted by an overwhelming majority voting in effect to go the way of the old time Baptists. They have provided five different ways for the churches to do their mission giving according to the desires of the congregations. The churches can now eliminate whatever SBC causes they choose and still give through the central mechanism of the state called the Cooperative Program. They have begun preparations to provide new literature for their churches, feeling that the national body's materials are inadequate. Texas Baptists have enlarged their own mission programs and provided additional avenues of theological education. In short, the changes nationally have produced radical changes in the way Texas Baptists are going to do their work.

One other serious effect of the upheaval has been the organization of a small dissident convention in Texas that vows to follow the ways of the new

SBC. A similar series of events has occurred in Virginia, resulting in a new dissident convention of churches. Other states have serious rifts, including North Carolina, Kentucky, Missouri, and Georgia.

## Evangelicals or Baptists

Curiously, the new SBC seems to be moving in a variety of ways closer to their fellow evangelicals while alienating many of their fellow Baptists:

- The Sunday School Board has changed its name to LifeWay Christian Resources of the Southern Baptist Convention. In doing so, the announcement was made that it wished to appeal to the larger "evangelical" market. The immediate protest quickly brought the statement that the materials would always be Baptistic. Many question whether this is true even now.
- The LifeWay Christian Resources recently announced a change in the names of its conference centers at Ridgecrest, N. C. and Glorieta, N. M. This was done in order to expand its market and to "collaborate with Evangelicals" in providing enlarged ministry. The well-known financial problems of the centers and the parent body in recent years are thought by many to be the driving force.
- The seminaries of the SBC are employing large numbers of new faculty members to replace those fired or resigned. Many of these new professors do not seem to have Southern Baptist educational backgrounds or experience in denominational schools. Customarily the announcement of new faculty appointments carries careful resumes of the church affiliation of the candidate as well as information about previous Baptist service or relationships. It is interesting to note that some have been elected recently without any of these data. A number of "presidential appointments" to seminary faculties have been made with no public information about educational or church backgrounds.
- A number of the new faculty has been educated in "evangelical" institutions with non- or interdenominational affiliations.
- Large numbers of students from other evangelical traditions are beginning to attend SBC institutions.
- The International Mission Board, the North American Mission Board, and the Ethics and Religious Liberty Commission have all announced that they are "collaborating" with other evangelicals in a variety of efforts in many arenas.

Kent Kellogg, a director of missions in Oklahoma, noted some of the potential problems:

I noticed co-sponsorship by four religious groups: Church of the Nazarene, United Methodist Church Board of Discipleship, Assemblies of God and LifeWay Christian Resources. The special guest is the pastor of a large Church of Christ in San Antonio, Texas. The purpose of the simulcast is to train pastors in principles of church growth. I applaud the effort, but must ask if we are sending mixed signals. (*Baptist Messenger*, April 1999)

Wayne Ward, retired professor from Southern Baptist Seminary, is even more specific in dealing with these problems:

Many of our Baptist leaders are emphasizing our kinship with American evangelicals much more than our distinctive heritage as Baptists....Baptists have never belonged to any of those "evangelical churches" which claim direct descent from one of the Protestant reformers, require adherence to a particular creed or, worst of all, seek political power to establish their church as a national church.

In order to join the circle of 'evangelical reformed theologians', embrace their schools and promote their books, Baptists are having to sell their birthright, namely such beliefs as the individual soul's direct access to God, freedom from political or religious coercion in all matters of faith, a free church in a free state and the supremacy of Scripture over all creeds, councils, confessions, conventions or religious authorities. (*Western Recorder*, February 1999)

Not all cooperation is bad, of course, and some will contribute to the work of the Lord. It undoubtedly inaugurates the largest effort at ecumenical cooperation in the history of the denomination. Perhaps vision will be enlarged and the work more effective. These citations are not intended to criticize evangelicals of whatever kind. Theirs is the same right to free choice as any Baptist.

There will be a new generation of evangelicals spawned out of these events. One question: Will they be Baptists? A second question: How is it possible that the SBC can cooperate with all these groups and not be able to accept their fellow Baptists who in fact built the organizations they co-opted?

The present SBC bears little resemblance to that which existed before 1979 and is rapidly departing from major principles called "Baptistic." Debaptistification is accelerating, power is concentrated, churches are disfranchised and thus individuals are free to practice their faith within the confines of the present structure or as some of the fundamentalist leaders have suggested get out!

# CHAPTER FIVE

# SOUL FREEDOM: SOIL FOR SEPARATION OF CHURCH AND STATE

## JAMES M. DUNN

William R. Estep wonders if some modern-day, nearly Baptists have a right to claim the name. Estep affirms "the separation of church and state, as the only sure guarantee of complete religious freedom, has been a Baptist conviction from the very beginning of the movement." He throws out this challenge:

> It is highly questionable whether one who rejects the principle of the institutional separation of church and state can consistently hold to religious freedom. If this is the case, can such a person legitimately claim to be a Baptist?

Estep contends, "Contemporary Baptists in the Southern Baptist Convention are uninformed regarding the unique heritage of Baptists." He has a point when the same misled denominational employees support a school prayer amendment to the United States Constitution, announce their intention to challenge "the strict separation of church and state," and file a friend of the court brief on behalf of vouchers for parochial schools.

The same revisionists working for the present fundamentalist leadership of the nation's largest Baptist body have trouble coming to terms with Baptist heritage. When the Southern Baptist agency, given religious liberty duties, published the denomination's historic statement on church-state relations, they felt that they had to amend it. Quoting Article 17 of *The Baptist Faith and Message,* they dropped these words: "the state has no right to impose taxes for the support of any form of religion." The simplest way to reconcile the fundamentalist practice with the Baptist confession of faith is to rewrite history. Baptists have found biblical warrant and have practiced consistent dedication to the principle of church-state separation as the sensible safeguard for soul freedom.

Where in the Bible is the separation of church and state taught? The question is asked. Sometimes the questioner is earnest and urgent. For those of us who take the Bible seriously, it is not a bad question. Jesus said, "Render therefore unto Caesar the things which are Caesar's; and unto God the things that are God's" (Matthew 22:21). That's a start. Jesus plainly spoke of a difference between what is God's and what is government's.

Then, there is no single proof text in the Bible on which to hang the Jeffersonian metaphor "a wall of separation between church and state." There are, however, biblical principles, theological presuppositions, historical examples, and pointed stories that form a firm foundation for keeping these two institutions distinct.

The biblical record leaves no doubt that all people are moral creatures. All human beings are response-able, responsible and free. The idea that humankind somehow replicates God requires this moral nature. Persons decide. Our "chooser" is close to our essential core. Soul freedom is universal.

Adam and Eve could want, wish, and will. Every wonderful "whosoever will" in scripture—from the capacity to choose at creation (Genesis 1) to the invitation in Revelation 22:17, "Whosoever will, let him take the water of life freely"—cries out for soul freedom.

That soul freedom marks the mystery of humanity: "A little lower than the angels" (Psalm 8:5) yet "there is none good, but one, God" (Mark 10:18). We are able to soar but apt to sink, capable of freedom but inclined to oppress.

Scripture also portrays us all as social beings. Our decisions and deeds have social consequences. This condition, individuals entangled in the lives of others, demands religious liberty. Joshua put it plainly to the children of Israel, "Choose you this day whom ye will serve;...but as for me and my house, we will serve the Lord." (Joshua 24:15). Jesus loved the rich young ruler but let him go away (Mark 10:17-22). The master did not lasso with a laser beam, tackle, or trip him. The appeal of Jesus requires decision. "Whosoever *will come* after me, *let* him *deny* himself, and *take up* his cross, and *follow* me." (Mark 8:34). That personal commitment cannot be made by anyone else. This is no proxy religion. There is one mediator between God and all humankind. That one is Jesus (I Timothy 2:5). Christians from the earliest church subscribed to the simple affirmation "Jesus is Lord." That puts followers of Jesus on an equal footing. The "law of liberty" further binds all believers to love one another, and this extends unto the "least of these" (Matthew 25:40).

The spiritual estimate of humankind shared by Jews and Christians sees us all as political animals. The Bible tells the stories of kings and generals, prophets and priests, good and bad government. The early church saw government *per se* as good, ordained by God (Romans 13), but potential as an instrument of evil (Revelation 13).

When one examines the records of civil disobedience, heroic martyrdom, and faithful witness, it is clear that churches closest to Jesus' day were not followers of a watered-down civil religion. No muddle-headed merger of God and country confused the church at first. They said with Peter, "We ought to obey God rather than men." (Acts 5:29). They understood that the ways of government were not the ways of God. "Not by might, nor by power, but by my spirit, saith the Lord of hosts." (Zechariah 4:6). Those first century Christians were too busy running *from* the Roman Senate to consider running *for* it but they did know the difference between church and state.

Baptists hold to the separation of church and state as the best guarantee for soul freedom.

Our *theology* demands it. Faith is appropriated personally; God's grace is experienced individually; one comes to Jesus Christ freely or not really; everyone must be free from the state's coercive powers in matters or religion.

Our *ethics* require it. If we do unto others as we want them to do unto us, if we believe that God loves the whole world, if we accept the image of God in every fellow human being, if we love our neighbors as ourselves, all people are entitled to real religious liberty.

Our *experience* commends it. The American experiment in church-state separation was in significant measure initiated by Baptists. Roger Williams, John Clarke, Isaac Backus, Samuel Stillman, John Leland, and others advanced this innovative relationship.

State religions are bad in principle. One can see the dangers and corruption of ties between church and state in Latin America, Ireland, and Iran. One can see the chaos and violence that attends state-supported religion in Lebanon, Sri Lanka, and Nepal. One can see the debilitating absence of conviction and vitality that accompanies an established church in England, Spain, and Sweden.

Yet, even today different dominant religions are actually pressing for recognition as the official national "church" in India, Poland, and Romania.

We warn against the tyrannies inherent in such arrangements. We affirm the spiritual value of the separation of church and state.

Believing in the separation of church and state doesn't make one a Baptist. But it is hard to believe that one could be a Baptist and not cling tenaciously to that baptistic doctrine. How else do we protect and defend those seminal beliefs in freedom of conscience, the priesthood of all believers, the right of private interpretation of Scripture, and real religious liberty for all believers as well as for those who refuse to believe? A free church in a free state is the device that best defends freedom.

Without these protections, how else can we insure the integrity of authentic evangelism, a prophetic witness, and an unhindered mission to share the whole gospel with whole people in the whole world?

A church in such close partnership with government that one cannot tell when worship leaves off and patriotism begins has slipped into idolatry. Without a healthy distance, the prophetic vision is blurred, the witness muffled and the gospel compromised.

Finally, when the church's mission is tinted, tainted, or tailored by the state, she has ceased to be the bride of Christ and fallen into an incestuous bed of cultural captivity.

Why is a sin-sick society so deaf to the Good News? One reason is clear. Too many Christians have been willing to let public institutions do too much of the church's job. The church has the marvelous assignment: "O Zion, haste thy mission high fulfilling; To tell to all the world that God is light; That he who made all nations is not willing; One soul should perish, lost in shades of night. Publish glad tidings; Tidings of peace; Tidings of Jesus; Redemption and release."

One reason that our wary forebears, whether sons of the enlightenment or children of the Puritan promise, insisted upon separation of church and state is their shared estimate of humankind. All peoples of The Book—Jews, Christians, and Muslims—did in days past hold a pessimistic perspective on human nature. They spoke of sin. The biblical formulas for original sin and total depravity crept into the common conversation of the most progressive religionists in colonial days. The deists, freethinkers, and even atheists could not communicate without appealing to "man's fallen nature." There was a healthy appreciation for human frailty.

Somehow there was a ring of truth from personal experience. When we have learned the truth, been shown the good, understood what is right, and seen clearly our own self-interest, we blow it. Who is so naive as to believe that if we know what's right we'll do it? That which we would, we do not. That which we would not, we do.

That's true of us as individuals, at least at times. It's truer of collections and collectives of individuals. Reinhold Niebuhr sized up sin in its social and political expression and let slip his conclusion in the title *Moral Man and Immoral Society.*

We will never forget. The holocaust took the measure of human hate and fear. It took place in the lifetime of many of us. Lebanon. Idi Amin. Kosovo. The words alone suggest a theological insight into corporate sin.

Is it any wonder that those founders who thought in religious constructs should insist on separation of church and state? Remember, Madison was a theologian at Witherspoon's fledgling Princeton. Jefferson, well taught in theology, could see, as Edwin Gaustad says, "...European history needlessly besmirched and tragically bloodied by the heavy hand of despotic religion."

The Baptist separationists, from Roger Williams and John Clarke through Isaac Backus and John Leland, trusted neither church nor state, because "all have sinned and come short of the glory of God." They were quite sure that the world was made up of two kinds of people, saved sinners and lost sinners, but sinners all, to be sure.

When the U. S. Congress was considering the exchange of ambassadors with a church, Kenneth W. Dam, an administration official, was asked at a public hearing why our State Department would want such an arrangement. He replied, "So the United States can influence the political policies of the Roman Catholic Church." The state influence policies of the church, indeed! Unfair. Out of bounds. A blatant violation of church-state separation.

Chief Justice of the Supreme Court, William Rehnquist, has said, "The 'wall of separation between church and state' is a metaphor based on bad history, a metaphor which proved useless as a guide to judging. It should be frankly and explicitly abandoned." Some of us believe that it is a metaphor rooted in good theology: "unto Caesar what is Caesar's, unto God what is God's"; that it has proved patently useful as the guarantor of liberty; that while it is not absolute, it is not obsolete; and that it should be treasured as a distinctive aspect of the American experiment. Can anyone possibly value soul freedom without seeing the need for a wall of separation between church and state?

Perhaps special care should be taken in the appointment of federal judges to inquire of their record on church-state issues. President Bush gave eloquent testimony to the vitality of his belief in the separation principle. He said:

Was I scared floating in a little yellow raft off the coast of an enemy-held island...? Of course I was. What sustains you in times like that? Well you go back to fundamental values. I thought about Mother and Dad and the strength I got from them—and God and faith in the separation of Church and State.

Useless metaphor? Surely everyone who shares Mr. Bush's faith in the separation of church and state will encourage and support this direction for the nation.

One think-tanker, Walter Berns, consistently advocates "a program of assistance on a non-discriminatory basis across the board, to all churches, all religion, all sects." How in the world does "fallen man" muster the wisdom, the will, the skill to dispense the limited public treasure to unlimited pluralistic religions and sects? How in heaven's name does imperfect government, tainted, scarred, effaced by sin, fairly relate to limited organized religion, self-admittedly made up of sorry sinners? No, it is ridiculous revisionism to think that the state can perform any religious function whatsoever. It is still sinful and tyrannical to take tax dollars by coercion, as is necessary, and divide them by any formula, however ingenious, among sects, religions, or belief systems.

Surely every conservative interested in preserving the tradition of church-state separation and every liberal dedicated to keeping heavy-handed government out of religion will stand behind any government safeguarding scarce tax dollars for truly public causes. Both liberals and conservatives should resist the statism that allows government to be the all in all. Close to the essence of sin in the biblical revelation is the pride in one's ability to go it alone, to do it himself, to mistake the creature for the creator. All of us understand on an intimate level Elton Trueblood's warnings against the "insufferable conceit, unbelievable self-righteousness" which resides in every heart. We may not yet have seen the utter folly in elaborate schemes that would mix and merge church and state in an inextricable embrace in charitable choice legislation that funds social programs in churches. We may not have understood the inevitable unfairness and injustice in exchanging ambassadors with one church. We may not have admitted to ourselves the ludicrous leap of logic in thinking that the common purse can provide even-handedly for our various faith-based programs.

Whether we call our limitations—recalcitrance, perversity and predicament—"sin," we'd better exercise the caution that takes it into account. The founders were not so stupid after all when they built into the structure all sorts of safeguards, including separation of church and state. Soul freedom is a treasure worth protecting.

CHAPTER SIX

# CONSERVATIVE CHRISTIANS
# AND THE RELIGIOUS RIGHT

GRADY C. COTHEN

*The Christian and the Social Order*
*Every Christian is under obligation to seek to make the will of Christ*
*supreme in his own life and in human society. Means and methods used*
*for the improvement of society and the establishment of righteousness*
*among men can be truly and permanently helpful only when they are*
*rooted in the regeneration of the individual by the saving grace of God in*
*Christ Jesus.*
*    ...In order to promote these ends Christians should be ready to work*
*with all men of good will in any good cause, always being careful to act*
*in the spirit of love without compromising their loyalty to Christ and His*
*truth."*

Baptist Faith and Message 1963

"Show respect for all men...treat them honorably." 1 Peter 2:17
(The Message)

In the 1980s a "Culture War" developed. As organized religion began to take
political sides on several issues, the fog thickened. Conservative groups, such
as the Southern Baptist Convention, and other evangelicals, Jews, and
Catholics, suddenly sounded like the protesters of the sixties and seventies.
Rifts developed between the new Religious Right and traditional denominationalists.

Religious leaders aligned with political parties and one could not tell
whether some meetings were political rallies or religious gatherings. Religious

groups that had refrained from overt political activity became involved with the agenda of organized political groups. Coalitions were formed between groups that had avoided each other. Common goals were spelled out for cooperation in political activity.

## Who is the Religious Right?

The Religious Right, including people like Jerry Falwell, Pat Robertson, Ralph Reed, James Dobson, and scores of other religious conservatives, led many religious organizations into the political maelstrom. They claimed superior morality, even thought some of their actions did not exhibit this behavior.

These prominent religious figures were joined in various matters by a variety of key politicians and conservative ideologues including Dick Armey, Tom DeLay, Trent Lott, Jesse Helms, Oliver North, Paul Weyrich, Joseph Coors, the DeVos of Amway, and reconstructionist R. J. Rushdoony.

The Religious Right often is financed and guided by a right-wing political group known as The Council For National Policy. A somewhat secretive group, they have withheld the names of their members until last year. There are several prominent Southern Baptist fundamentalist leaders on this council. While these men would not be considered wealthy when compared to other council members, Southern Baptists include Jerry Falwell, Page Patterson, Jay Strack, and Coy Privette. Paul Pressler and Jesse Helms apparently are the only two with any substantial wealth.

White evangelicals comprise almost 25 percent of registered voters. This is about three times the number of African-American voters, four times the number of non-religious voters, and 12 times the number of Jewish voters. Approximately one-fourth to one-third of the evangelicals openly identify with the Religious Right. Rice Professor William Martin discovered that the Right dominates the Republican Party in at least 18 states with substantial influence in 13 others (William Martin, "The Christian Right," *Foreign Policy* Spring 1999).

With approximately 200 "Christian" television stations and 1,400-1,500 "Christian" radio stations, there is a formidable political force at work. As various evangelical groups and prominent individuals coalesced around such causes as the opposition to abortion, homosexuality, and control of school boards, political activity and conflict intensified.

Many evangelical Christians were caught between the Religious Right and their opponents. These Christians sometimes agreed with the basic moral stand of the Right, but opposed the way the Religious Right intermingled politics and religion. Likewise, they did not always approve of the people they chose as allies.

## Conservative Christians or Religious Right?

Thus, two distinct evangelical groups emerged in the 80s: Conservative Christians and the Religious Right. These groups had many similarities:

• Most members would claim belief in an inspired Bible.
• Often they wanted the same outcomes such as end of abortion.
• Frequently they would agree on what was right and wrong.
• Both groups wanted righteousness in public life.
• Both held reverence for human life.
• There was a common desire for justice, though they would frequently disagree on what it was and how obtained.
• Personal integrity was important in private and public life.

Thus, while these groups often shared the same basic convictions they differed strongly on how to achieve their goals.

While the Religious Right and other Conservative Christians agreed on many moral principles and goals, there were vast differences: for example, the difference in attitude toward the sinners of society, the methods for reaching social goals, views of the opposition groups, and especially the attitude adopted toward those who disagreed.

Most basic, perhaps, was the use of the Bible in the conflict. The Religious Right sought scriptural justification for the stands they took on issues. The theological methodology was known as "proof texting." They found a passage that seemed to confirm their point and used it to support their position. Since the Bible by poor hermeneutics (interpretation) can be made to mean almost anything, they had little trouble justifying whatever was demanded.

George Marsden correctly labels the Religious Right as fundamentalist. Even Southern Baptist leader James Draper, before he joined the Southern Baptist fundamentalists in taking over the convention, called fundamentalism the most dangerous heresy of our time. He said the fundamentalist is:

[Any person who] feels he has a corner on truth; his approach is virtually always negative and condemning; there is no room in his world for those who have a different persuasion. He has a divisive spirit, is unfair and his tactic is simple: hatred, bitterness, and condemnation of all whom they despise.

## Are the methods used by the Religious Right appropriate Christian behavior?

One basic characteristic of the RR is *judgmentalism*. One gets the impression from their performances that they believe they know what is right—for everyone. Other opinions or points of view are of little concern except as they plan to overcome them.

This approach to legislating Christian principles raises many problems and questions as to the freedom of religion, academic freedom, and the rights of the minority or majority dissenters.

Their legalistic interpretations of Scripture and religious truth create many problems in dealing with their arguments. A Scripture passage must be interpreted literally.

Thus, they project the ability to know God into absolutist conclusions: "This is what God said—to me or us—this is what I think, so this is what is right. We have the right to judge right and wrong because of our understanding of the revelation. If this is right, then we have the right to enforce our understanding. To question us is to question the revelation of the Will of God."

In evangelical understanding, since God made man in his image—with freedom of choice—the Will of God is never imposed by human instrumentality. Suddenly, in free America, we have those who seem to assume they are capable of imposing the Will of God on others.

Another characteristic of the RR is their method of conflict resolution. The only method they use is confrontation! Likely these attitudes spring from the above-mentioned confidence that they know what God wants. Calm dialogue and consensus mean they have compromised their position. Negotiation is weakness or even wickedness to the RR.

Another descriptive term of the Religious Right is *aggressiveness*. Once a decision is reached on the "right" course, action is required and a plan to dominate their opposition begins. Many school districts in the country are in turmoil because of this approach.

## Methods of the Religious Right

(1) Organization is a key factor in their success. The lessons of precinct politics were learned early and applied to every level of interest. The conflicts in the local school districts, report cards on legislators they reject, the enlistment of pastors and churches to distribute their propaganda, their presence in political organizations, their lobbying at every level of government, and many

other efforts illustrate the point. They are often masters at propagandizing and polarizing.

(2) A major tactic of the RR is the use of power. Contrary to the religious heritage of many of them, power in achieving their goals is not only legitimate but also mandatory. They believe in creationism over evolution and so they use the power of the ballot to elect school board members who will use the power of the office to require teaching of creationism.

They reject abortion—even if it is legal—and use the power of public harassment to intimidate women, doctors, and the owners of clinics. These public scenes of near or complete hysteria have resulted in deaths from clinic bombings. The RR denies their participation in these unfortunate events, but the hysteria was in large measure created by such groups.

(3) The use of the majority rule principle has been honed to a fine edge by the RR. "If enough votes can be garnered to win the issue on the ballot, we win and we have the votes to prove it." As a matter of political philosophy, this is a proper view. When it comes to the matters of religious conscience on any issue, this is not appropriate. The requirement to teach a particular religious idea or require prayer in public school that offends the conscience of the minority illustrates the problem. Early in the history of this country the religious forbears of the present RR were a minority. The official opinion differed significantly from theirs and as a result a substantial number were jailed and beaten for religious dissidence.

(4) Force and intimidation have become the tools of bringing societal change. Many of the changes are matters of religious belief or personal conscience—for example, abortion, homosexuality, school prayer, school curricula, vouchers for religious schools, and display of religious symbols. The RR is quite willing to go to the mat to achieve their goals in these and many other matters, regardless of the conscience of others.

The sometimes-extreme positions are particularly problematic. The Coalition opposes separation of church and state, about which Pat Robertson said on television: "There is no such thing in the Constitution. It's a lie of the Left, and we're not going to take it anymore." He has also repeatedly attacked the public schools in intemperate terms and called for replacing them with religious academies. The Istook amendment, had it been adopted, would have permitted government officials to lead prayers in classrooms, courtrooms, and various other "captive audience settings." It would have permitted individual states to declare themselves officially "Christian."

The Christian Coalition's request for federal tax-exempt status has been denied. The organization, founded by Pat Robertson, has been accused of opposing and supporting candidates for office through its voter guides, delivered days before federal elections.

(5) One of the more serious trends in the RR is the attempt to use civil (government) power to achieve religious ends. Religious issues related to the public school system illustrate the problem. Bible reading or study, prayer and/or the teaching of religious dogma, however good, creates impossible situations for those of different religious persuasions.

The use of civil authority to achieve religious goals raises the specter of civil religion. Religion controlled by the state according to a system of law or even custom will bear little or no relationship to true religious experience. True religious experience is that between a person and God, or in some cases between the person and the church. In neither can a true religious transaction occur at the behest of civil authority.

Richard Land of the Southern Baptist Convention believes that morality can be legislated. He is likely referring to such things as the abolition of abortion by law and laws against murder. A closer examination will reveal that laws may have prevented some acts of violence but certainly have not stopped them. Of course, society must be protected from many types of conduct. Whether law can control moral decisions is highly questionable.

(6) Much of the present controversy revolves around the RR trying to use the rule of a minority conscience to control majority social conduct. That much going on in our society offends the conscience of the RR (and Conservative Christians) is evident to all. It is equally obvious that what offends Christians of either variety does not offend others. Whose conscience is to rule? Certainly all parties to the social contract should and must have the right to contend for their positions in lawful ways. To impose the view of a minority on all because of superior organization or finances or political power is neither democratic nor free exercise of religion.

(7) So perhaps the most-often heard complaint concerning the RR is that they are trying to impose their beliefs on others. Despite fervent denial the efforts go on to do precisely that. Only recently have some of the groups begun to search for alternatives to abortion and evangelism efforts for homosexuals.

The Religious Right in many ways seems to be the Puritans of the twentieth century. They have the same sometimes-fierce determination to dominate the religious scene and secure public conformity to their views of how things should be. The move to partner with government at any level to secure these ends sounds curiously like the early Puritans who believed it was acceptable for the government to enforce religious beliefs so long as the beliefs conformed to their own.

The exclusiveness of the RR is a source of many conflicts. One either subscribes to their agenda or is declared the enemy. The SBC has a particularly questionable record in this regard. Adjunct professors at one seminary were recently disqualified from teaching because one had attended a session of a Cooperative Baptist Fellowship state meeting and another had "a connection" with the organization. The national body forbids any church member to serve on any national committee or board if the church supports the Fellowship financially. The leaders who enforce this policy led their churches in giving to many outside causes before they came to power in the SBC. Present SBC leaders vigorously supported such non-denominational causes as Mid America Seminary, Criswell Bible College, Luther Rice Seminary, Liberty University, and many other such ventures.

## Christian-Bashing

This kind of conduct among the RR has, of course, produced resistance and vigorous protest in many places by many groups. The criticism from prominent and influential sources is beginning to produce its own reaction. The RR is becoming more and more sensitive to the criticism that in some cases rivals their own attacks on others. Some of the RR are now accusing of religious persecution those who object to their efforts.

Richard Land of the SBC Ethics Commission recently reacted in his sermon to the national body. He said that Christians in America are being targeted by a persistent campaign to exclude them from the halls of government and the public square. He cautioned that:

> [There is a] conscious, concerted, clever attempt by the various ruling elite in this country—the legal elite, the business elite, the social elite, the economic elite and even some religious elite—to marginalize Christians and to drive them from involvement in the public policy of this nation...we must tell them we will no longer allow them to censor and suppress us and to keep us from our rightful place in the public square. (*BP*, June 1997)

Cal Thomas, for years an ardent supporter of rightist causes on the political agenda, recently wrote in *Newsweek* that the cause is dispirited, even despondent:

> Politics has failed to deliver what we thought it promised. Conservative Christians are increasingly frustrated that the cultural viruses of abortion and drugs have proved largely immune to political inoculation...the

establishment GOP is now trying to distance itself from its believing base. Meanwhile, true believers—including me—are beginning to sense that the kingdom of this world, which regularly demands compromise, cannot be reconciled to a kingdom not of this world that allows for no compromise...His (Jesus) is not a realm that needs soldiers to establish or defend it...It is since Christians have largely ceased to think of the other world that they have become so ineffective in this one. Aim at Heaven and you will get earth 'thrown in'. Aim at earth and you get neither.

## Conservative Christians

The conservative Christians under consideration here will have varied opinions about many matters of faith. They begin with some simple but profound religious presuppositions. They begin with a Biblical faith. They believe that man is capable of knowing God, that God can communicate with him, that God has a purpose for mankind, and that He will help individuals and groups to fulfill that purpose. Christ was sent to the earth as the principal part of the Father's effort at redemption of persons from evil. Faith in Christ is the connecting point between man and God. Each person is responsible for herself or himself and the decisions of life. Yet, the Christian has a social responsibility to be a good citizen and participate individually in societal decision making.

While many of the RR subscribe to this brief summary of beliefs, the methods, motives, and manner of conduct of the Conservative Christians is significantly different.

Change for these people is not to be wrought by "war for Christ" since He was not a person of war. They begin with a Biblical theology. This system of beliefs is based on an effort to determine the whole truth of Scripture on any given subject. Proof-texting won't satisfy the genuine Christian student.

While they might organize to lobby for some societal change, the methodology is seriously different. First, they believe it is the message of God and his love that changes people for good and for the good. Changes in society are in the long run produced by changes in persons. Changed persons produce institutional change.

The tools of this community of believers in societal change are the tools of education, reason, negotiation, dialogue, and consensus on non-Biblical positions. The tools of individual change are the truth of Scripture, the influence of God in the human heart and the proper response of the individual to God's initiative.

In short, these Christians hold to the notion—perceived by others to be naive—that the proclamation of the message of God's love accompanied by their godly living and giving of self in His service is the way to go to reach people with a message of reason and love. No one is permitted to interfere with their practice of their faith following their own conscience. Fellow Christians in the church and other fellowships support the faith stance.

Others have the same rights and their consciences are valid for them. Coercion of any sort is viewed as wrong. The use of power or force or undue influence on the conscience of others is rejected.

Of course, some controls by government are essential for the public good and protection. These should be tested by the public welfare and avoid interference with the practice of religious faith unless the practice infringes on the rights and welfare of others.

Mark Wingfield of the *Western Recorder* recently wrote: "When we attempt to control the world, we deny the power of Jesus to change the world. Jesus did not operate from a position of power, but of love. If we really believe what he taught, we ought to shun power and seek love as well" (June 1997).

One significant point for the Christian in this group is that judgment of the conscience of others is the responsibility of God. To be sure, this dictum is observed in the violation as much as in the practice far too often. The reservation of judgment of others is often taught in Scripture and its observance would eliminate many of the controversies of the present time.

This is not to say that these people do not abhor wrong, speak out against it, and work to replace wrong with right. It is to say that they have an obligation to show the love of God toward sinners if not their sin. They often believe that the methods and rhetoric of the RR breed hatred and schism.

Further the CC is concerned with spiritual insight, divine help, self-discipline, love, and help for others. If their living and message are rejected, others have the same rights as they and have a perfect right to believe or not to believe as they choose. No coercion is permitted. If force of any kind is used, the result will not be a valid spiritual decision.

Both groups have many individuals who disagree with abortion. The CC would prefer to deal with the basic problems producing the practice. When it is time for an abortion, it is usually too late to deal with the basic problems behind it. Most of the CC would not likely join the frenzied group of protesters but would seek help for the victim.

The attempt to describe such divergent and diverse groups of people as simply Conservative Christians probably idealizes them and their beliefs. It is also possible that some of the criticism of the RR unduly categorizes some improperly. Again, it must be remembered that individuals and some groups migrate from group to group depending on the issue of the moment.

## Some Substantive Issues

These discussions pose in perhaps too simple a form some basic issues involved in societal change and free exercise of religion.

All of the issues of separation of church and state have come again to center-stage. How much invasion of the state by the church can be tolerated without the decimation of the minorities? How can major religious causes be accommodated without equal accommodation to every "minor" group? How much practice of religious ritual, symbol, and presence in public ceremony is permissible in the world's most pluralistic society? How much interference by a special-interest religious group, however good the intent, can be tolerated in the governmental arena without the chaos of the entry of all the combatants into the same arena?

Correspondingly, how much state interference with religious practice can be tolerated in the name of public well-being? With Congress, the judiciary, and the state legislatures tinkering with the various mechanisms that relate to public expression of religion, when does free exercise suffer? Can governmental entities set rules that recognize the dominant religious groups without equal treatment under the law for all? The issues here have multiplied the dockets in dozens of courts at all levels. The present controversies are intensifying the church-state conflicts exponentially.

Another substantive issue is, how is civic order to be achieved? By law, majority power, coercion of public opinion? It is obvious that protection of society from many forms of harm is the business of government. What of the place of individual and social righteousness—honesty, sexual responsibility, equal treatment of all citizens, concern for the poor, health care for all?

The march toward the supreme rightness of majority rule poses serious problems. Is the majority always right? Certainly the majority determines elections, but does that mean that it is always right? What of the minorities? Not very long ago Baptists were minorities, Catholics were unwelcome in some places, Jews were outcasts, Muslims weren't a force in America, and Mormons were run out of town and state. Each of these groups is equally certain of the correctness of their positions on religious and many civic issues. Can the RR or the Christian Coalition be allowed to penalize these and others?

When Christianity was first tolerated and finally embraced by government in the fourth century, it began a slide into the dark ages. For more than a thousand years the church and the state(s) were in constant competition for control. When religion beds down with politics, the offspring are renegades. Religion is always contaminated. Politics manipulates religion, using its language, traditions, and power to achieve political advantage. Usually religion is misrepresented and its reputation inevitably suffers.

Political methodology is used by religion to attain its goals and the result is less than religious (at least less than Christian). If religion manipulates the political establishment for its own purposes, the political process is contaminated and must constantly shift its stand to placate its many adherents.

The present conflict between the Religious Right and the many institutions of society is leaving behind a swath of the wounded, scandalized, and misrepresented. While some good may come of the conflict, one of the groups most put upon is the great mass of Conservative Christians who may believe in the cause but deplore the motive and the method.

The great issue that continues to rise out of the rubble is soul freedom. Many of the tactics of the political adversaries on both sides of some of these contests threaten the rights of a minority or of individuals. Social righteousness rises from below; it is not handed down from above. The nation must not lose its distinctiveness of freedom of conscience for all while seeking to make religious decisions in the ballot box.

# CHAPTER SEVEN

# CHURCH, STATE, AND SOUL FREEDOM

## JAMES M. DUNN

The concept of "soul competency" or "soul freedom" is as timely as today's newspapers. A *Newsweek* story about Tony Campolo illustrates the relevance of this Baptist belief. "Campolo believes in 'soul competency,' the Baptist doctrine which holds that each individual has the ability to find in the Bible the answers he is seeking."

This timeless tenet recently has sparked new interest among sociologists, as evidenced by Robert N. Bellah's address at the American Academy of Religion on November 22, 1997. Bellah said:

> What was so important about the Baptists, and other sectarians such as the Quakers, was the absolute centrality of religious freedom, of the sacredness of individual conscience in matters of religious belief. Why our society is so hospitable to the ideology, if not the reality of multiculturalism is best traced to our passion for that principle.

Harold Bloom, in an important book in 1992, *The American Religion*, named E. Y. Mullins one of America's seminal theologians:

> Edgar Young Mullins I would nominate as the Calvin or Luther or Wesley of the Southern Baptists, but only in the belated American sense, because Mullins was not the founder of the Southern Baptists but their re-founder, the definer of their creedless faith. An endlessly subtle and original religious thinker. Mullins is the most neglected of major American theologians. Pragmatically, he is more important than Jonathan Edwards, Horace Bushnell, and the Niebuhrs, because Mullins reformulated (perhaps even first formulated) the faith of a major American denomination. (Harold

Bloom, *The American Religion*, New York: Simon & Schuster 1992, 199)

Bloom, the eminent literary critic, attributes the teaching of "soul competency" to E. Y. Mullins:

> I have tried...to find some instance of the phrase 'soul competency' before Mullins, but...[have not] uncovered it in Southern Baptist writing or anywhere else. Mullins invented it, and slyly made no fuss about this, but employed it as though it were traditional and as old as the Baptists themselves, or indeed as old as Christianity. It is what John Milton called Christian Liberty.

Mullins was both "Northern" and "Southern" Baptist. He ranged from Andover Newton to Louisville. He invested energy and meaning in the phrase, placed it at the center of a coherent cluster of beliefs that define Baptists, and explored its religious, social, and political implications.

## Soul Competency Assessed

Karl Barth, in an interview with Louie D. Newton in 1955, credited Mullins with invention of the phrase: "How I thank God for Mullins and Broadus and Conner. Mullins gave the world a mighty phrase—the competency of the soul."

H. Wheeler Robinson, British Baptist theologian, deferred to Mullins for the definition of Baptist principles.

> The Biblical significance of the Baptists is the right of private interpretation [of], and obedience to, the Scriptures. The significance of the Baptists in relation to the individual is soul freedom, a regenerated church-membership and the equality and priesthood of believers. The political significance of Baptists is the separation of church and state. However, as comprehending all of the above particulars, as a great and aggressive force in Christian history, as distinguished from all others and standing entirely alone, the doctrine of the soul's competency in religion under God is the distinctive significance of the Baptists. (H. Wheeler Robinson, *The Life and Faith of Baptists*, London: The Kingsgate Press 1946, 24)

Robert Torbet, with others, credited Mullins' with a "new Baptist apologetic," one implemented "by an emphasis upon the accessibility of God to all men and the free responsibility of each individual before God, hence a free church in a free state." Torbet links the soul competency concept directly with the essence of Mullins' political ethic. (See E. Y. Mullins, Why Christianity is so True, Chicago: Christian Culture Press 1905, 352-353.)

John R. Sampey referred to Mullins' principle of the competency of the soul under God in religion as "the mother principle." God refuses to violate man's moral nature even to save him. Sampey made the connection between the "soul competency" and the separation of church and state. "Baptists today oppose the appropriation of public money for sectarian schools, and the enforced reading of the Bible in the public schools." That was in 1908.

Yet, for all the consensus, the historical consequence of Mullins' theology may well lie in his contribution to the current conflict in Baptist thought. Keen insights come from an outsider.

Harold Bloom, often called "America's most distinguished literary critic," sees Mullins' concept of "soul competency destroying fundamentalism." Since "sanctioning endless interpretive possibilities…the weird metaphor of a 'literal' or 'inerrant' reading totally vaporizes."

For Bloom, consequences lie far beyond Baptists, religion, or even "political, socioeconomic and anthropological implications." If the vision of soul freedom is lost, also the stance of John Milton and Roger Williams, then more than our spiritual democracy will be threatened.

## Soul Competency Described

If, indeed, soul freedom is the hallmark of Baptists (and for that matter of any civilized, biblical religion), what is it? It is simply the freedom, ability, and responsibility of each person to respond to God for herself or himself. A few phrases draw a picture of soul freedom:

• God's ability to communicate a revelation to human beings and their capacity to receive it and to communicate with God.
• The emphasis upon personality and personal responsibility—the nature of saving faith, a personal relation to Christ.
• The sinner's response to the gospel message is an act of moral freedom. Coercion here, as elsewhere in the moral realm, would destroy the highest element in human nature.
• In His assertion of the autonomy and independence of religion, Jesus thereby declares the freedom and autonomy of all forms of human culture.
• The capacity to deal directly with God.
• Voluntarism is nothing but a new name, scientifically and psychologically wrought with great care, for a very old and very profound word: faith.

Mullins did act out of profound presuppositions about the obvious clarity of the biblical revelation regarding soul freedom.

The voluntary principle is at the heart of Christianity. The right of private judgment in religion is a right that lies at the core of Christian truth. Objections to the doctrine of soul competency do seem strange to those whose religion is both biblical and experiential. Soul freedom makes sense. Grady Cothen concurs that soul freedom is axiomatic, a self-evident truth that when seen needs no proof of its reality.

He quotes approvingly Scott Walker, who says, "For me, to be a Baptist is to claim the privilege and the freedom of being your own theologian and your own interpreter of Scripture."

Walter B. Shurden says that if one accepts biblical authority, the appeal of Baptists to soul freedom is anchored in (1) the nature of God, (2) the nature of humanity, and (3) the nature of faith. God who dared to create us as free beings is portrayed in the Bible as a liberating Deity. Created in the image of God, a human being is the crowning work of God's creation....To deny freedom of conscience to any person is to debase God's creation. To be authentic, faith must be free.

Bill J. Leonard echoes the same understanding of soul competency: a belief for which no proof is necessary for the believer and no proof is possible for the unbeliever.

Leon McBeth responds in the same way, citing an evangelistic evidence of soul freedom. Every Gospel invitation implies the freedom of people to accept Christ as Savior. Every profession of faith in Christ implies that the convert has the power to decide for Christ.

Every commitment to Christian service implies that the person has competence to hear God's call and freedom to accept it. Competent persons have the necessary ability to consider alternatives and make decisions, and God has given every person the ability and the necessity to decide.

## Soul Competency Criticized

Critics of "soul freedom" see in it unbounded individualism, unlimited optimism, theological subjectivism, and faith without authority. Some fear a tendency to make every man's hat his own church.

Yet, could any one contend that it is clearly apparent that this principle was derived from the general cultural, political, and religious climate of the nineteenth century rather than based on biblical sources? Yes, "soul competency" is "derived," but it is a small leap for biblical warrant.

Theology is an interpretation of religion. It is a matter of experience. Direct, first-hand knowledge of God and acquaintance with God is possible. Theology is not merely a system of philosophy or abstract intellectualism.

## Religious Freedom and Soul Freedom

This concept of soul freedom is the ultimate source of all modern notions of human rights. Quakers and Baptists as the radical sects of the Protestant Reformation advanced this view of religious freedom. Such freedom of conscience may be the oldest "right of man"—as Jellinek has argued convincingly, at any rate it is the most basic right of man because it comprises all ethically conditioned action and guarantees freedom from compulsion, especially from the power of the state.

Religious liberty, the basic human right, is universal in its appeal and application. As Mullins said, Baptists believe in religious liberty for themselves. But they believe in it equally for all. While we have no sympathy with atheism, agnosticism, or materialism, we stand for the freedom of the atheists, agnostics, and materialists in their religious or non-religious convictions.

The connection between soul freedom and church-state separation should be obvious. When the heavy hand of government, inevitably coercive, enters the realm of religion, it always diminishes personal freedom.

Religion is a personal matter between the soul and God. Simply set out, soul competency is accessible to all. It must include the doctrine of church and state separation, said Mullins, in his watershed address to the Baptist World Alliance in 1923:

Religious liberty excludes:
• State authority in religion
• The principle of toleration in religion
• The right of the State to impose taxes for the support of one form of religion
• The imposition of creeds by ecclesiastical authority
• Centralized ecclesiastical government....

   To put the power and prestige of the State behind one form of religion and merely tolerate others is not religious liberty....

   Religious liberty was as nearly absolute as any safeguarded by the constitutions or practiced as natural right without protections of law.

## Soul Freedom and the State

Politically driven historical revisionists contend today that church-state separation is a myth. The fact of separation overshadows the political process. Church and state have distinct constituencies, purposes, methods, and sources of funding. The coercive powers of the state alone make for church-state separation. The Church must never usurp the rights of the State, must never seize the sword, and must always propagate the truth through love and sacrifice. The Church is a voluntary organization; the State compels obedience. One organization is temporal; the other spiritual. The direct allegiance in the Church is to God; in the State, it is to law and government. One is for the protection of life and property; the other is for the promotion of spiritual life. Mullins links soul freedom to his political ethic:

> For its own ends the state is sovereign. However, those ends do not include the religious life of the individual at all. Hence, the civil and religious life of persons belongs to different spheres entirely. The right of every soul to direct access to God is an inalienable right, with which the state must not interfere.

Romans 13:1-7; Matthew 22:21; Acts 5:29; Matthew 10:28; Matthew 23:10; Romans 14:4; John 4: 23, 24. That Baptist of the essence, Mullins, saw the social implications of soul freedom:

> Equality of individual worth carries with it the necessary implication that no man should be crowded to the wall from lack of opportunity. The powerful should be restrained and held within proper limits...the cunning or wise or mighty individual shall not ruthlessly crush his feebler brother for 'in the image of God created he him.' (E. Y. Mullins, *Why Christianity Is True*, Chicago: Christian Culture Press, 1905, 352, 353)

Separation of church and state does not mean separation of God from government or separation of Christians from citizen duties or politics from religion. Gardner Taylor calls for some distance between the institutions of government and religion "so the church will have some swinging room." Mullins opposed using the public schools for "enforced" Bible reading and he opposed "appropriation of public money for sectarian schools."

He also opposed "creationism" and called on the churches to be careful not to "resort to civil power to carry on its work." Alas, some modern Baptists pursue the use of civil power to do the work of the church, posting the Ten Commandments in classrooms and attacking all ears with so-called "school prayer."

## Soul Freedom and the Spirit of the Times

Soul freedom is the fueling engine for all progress. It is the constant in a social ethic with intellectual liberty, aesthetic liberty, economic liberty, political liberty, and religious liberty.

Sadly, Bloom's jeremiad about the disappearance of authentic Baptists seems all too true in this regard. Mullins' optimism seems naive about the triumph of soul competency, spiritual religion, and creedless Christianity among Baptists. Yet, one never knows enough to be totally pessimistic. God is still on the throne.

A common-sense faith that is accessible to every soul is ever eagerly sought. Soul freedom is most fundamentally in accord with the ongoing of the world toward democracy, and it would be calamitous to the social and political development of the world should Baptists abandon their own ideals.

# CHAPTER EIGHT

# FREEDOM AND HIGHER EDUCATION

### GRADY C. COTHEN

*Education*
*The cause of education in the Kingdom of Christ is co-ordinate with the*
*causes of missions and general benevolence, and should receive along with*
*these the liberal support of the churches. An adequate system of Christian*
*schools is necessary to a complete spiritual program for Christ's people.*

*In Christian education, there should be a proper balance between*
*academic freedom and academic responsibility. Freedom in any orderly*
*relationship of human life is always limited and never absolute.*

*The Baptist Faith and Message,* 1963

"...And the truth will make you free." John 8:32

The catastrophic collision between fundamentalism and higher education has
been too little noted but long will be remembered. Few areas of Baptist life
have been so drastically affected as the institutions of higher learning.

## Theological Education

Before the "conservative resurgence," theological education among Southern
Baptists was judged by most observers to be alive and well. The years since
World War II had witnessed enormous growth; three new schools were
organized and supported. Unparalleled progress was made in the number of
students, faculty, and physical facilities and in resources and recognition. The
system had produced six quite different kinds of institutions. They were
scattered from North Carolina to California.

As expected, the schools were providing a long line of pastors, church staff persons, missionaries, and professors. Their primary objective was not theological elitism but the training of servant church leaders. In the intervening years, the schools were gaining academic competence and sometimes excellence. All were accredited by their peers through the appropriate accrediting agencies. For a number of years, the schools enrolled about 20 percent of all theological students in America. Southern Baptists were less than 10 percent of the population.

By theological academic standards, all were classified as theologically conservative. At times, the schools were somewhat constrained by some of their ultra-conservative fellow Baptists. It is worthwhile to note that for many years less than half of Southern Baptist pastors had a theological education. It was inevitable that this, together with a worldwide resurgence of fundamentalism, would cause problems for any system of theological education. As a result, the schools were often indicted but seldom convicted of theological liberalism. Now and again some adventurous idea gained currency, or a young theologian tried to "contribute," or a student thought he knew more than the professor did and the theological fat was in the fire.

It is fair to say that paralleling the unprecedented development of the system of theological education there were those who longed for a different approach. It is interesting to note that the present-day leaders of the Southern Baptist Convention were during these years students making waves. When they became pastors the waves grew in size and volume. Accusations against some professors were frequent but real theological liberalism was minimal.

During the years, following the creation of Golden Gate, Midwestern and Southeastern seminaries there arose a small but vigorous theological education movement suited to fundamentalism. The dissatisfaction with the SBC system or the lack of attaining the leadership positions of control caused a small number of able leaders to turn elsewhere for theological training. W. A. Criswell of Dallas First Baptist Church began his own school that became Criswell College. A dissident professor and Home Mission Board employee began Mid-America Seminary and located it in Memphis. What many called a correspondence school, Luther Rice Seminary, began and the number of young pastors with doctorates appeared in many places. Jerry Falwell organized a theological seminary.

Critics of the SBC seminaries supported these schools. Current SBC leaders were among those "in competition with the SBC." (The fundamentalist leadership complains about the numbers of new theological schools that are compatible with the Cooperative Baptist Fellowship.)

When the so-called conservative resurgence or fundamentalist landslide swept the denomination, the educational system became fractured.

Paul Pressler attracted a lot of publicity with his attacks on the seminaries. He said that he spoke hundreds of times in many places concerning "liberalism in the seminaries." He published a paper of more than 50 pages quoting various professors that was supposed to substantiate his charges. Most of the objections had to do with interpretation or persons not teaching in a seminary, but the mud stuck in the minds of many. A few of his charges were made against the Sunday School Board. All but one or two matters of substance had been dealt with long before he made his accusations.

A serious turning point occurred with the report of the Peace Committee appointed by the Convention in 1985, which tried to resolve the controversy in the denomination. After two years and several attempts at finding common ground, the seminary presidents had formulated a statement (the Glorieta Statement) that was designed to reassure Southern Baptists that the seminaries were on the right track. The statement affirmed the miracles of the Bible, the full inspiration of Scripture and its binding authority, and the statement, "the sixty-six books of the Bible are not errant in any area of reality."

This effort gave some comfort to the fundamentalists on the committee but strong disagreement by others. The most crucial segment of the final report had to do with the nature of the Bible from a fundamentalist point of view. The confessional statement of *The Baptist Faith and Message* of 1963 said: "The Bible is truth without any mixture of error." The committee interpreted *The Baptist Faith and Message* passage on the Bible as they asserted Southern Baptists believed it. The committee said:

(1) They (Southern Baptists) believe in direct creation and therefore they believe Adam and Eve were real persons.
(2) They believe the named authors did indeed write the biblical books attributed to them....
(3) They believe all the miracles described in Scripture did indeed occur as supernatural events in history.
(4) They believe the historical narratives are accurate and reliable....

One watershed event of the controversy occurred when the Peace Committee said:

We call upon Southern Baptist institutions to recognize the great number of Southern Baptists who believe in this interpretation of our confessional statement and, in the future, to build their professional staffs and faculties

> from those who clearly reflect such dominant convictions and beliefs held
> by Southern Baptists at large. ("First Day" Part II, *SBC Bulletin* 1987, p. 12)

Here was a careful official interpretation of a confessional statement, a strange and unprecedented step for Baptists.

This overriding demand for uniformity and conformity according to the vote of the parent body would have a profound affect on the future of the denomination. Other parts of the document were soon forgotten, such as the call for "fairness in the appointive process" which was never even attempted. The instruction to adhere to given interpretations of Scripture has been front and center for a decade.

The denominational creed had taken on formal character. Every seminary professor was on notice to stand up and deliver according to prescription. While the fundamentalists had been crying for "parity" (equal numbers of fundamentalists and "liberals"), immediately the cry changed to "surgery is required in the seminaries."

Even before the Peace Committee report, the fundamentalists had the votes to force the denomination to conform to their will. Southern Baptist Theological Seminary, Southeastern, and Midwestern seminaries headed their list for reform.

## Southeastern Baptist Theological Seminary

Trustee pressure quickly caused Southeastern to change the method of faculty selection, elect fundamentalist sympathizers as trustees and officers, and begin to press for a complete overhaul of the institution. Unfamiliarity with institutional documents soon ran them aground of accreditation principles but did not deter them from securing the resignation of the president. Soon after, the Southern Association of Colleges and Schools and the Association of Theological Schools sent representatives to Southeastern for an account.

Today only two of the original 38 faculty members remain.

## Southern Baptist Theological Seminary

The problems took a slightly different turn at Southern Seminary. Strong attacks were made on the faculty and particularly President Roy Honeycutt. (See *What Happened to the Southern Baptist Convention?* for a full discussion of the circumstances.) After a series of capable defenses of the faculty and institutional life, President Honeycutt retired.

The trustees elected Albert Mohler, a young doctoral graduate of the seminary. He was an avid supporter of the fundamentalist resurgence and immediately began to purge Southern Seminary.

Amid much publicity and considerable reaction, he declared himself a "five point Calvinist." He set out to prove that the school was founded by people of like persuasion.

He wrote at length, questioning the conclusions of E. Y. Mullins, Southern Seminary's best-known theologian. Mullins had enormous influence in the SBC for more than half a century and gave prominence to the idea of soul competency before God. Mullins' ideas disturbed Mohler, who thought that he over-emphasized individualism and autonomy.

In a recent convocation address, Mohler said that the common worldview, which once guided the founders of the American Republic, has been jettisoned and replaced with:

> ...the shapeless void of rights-talk and naked self-interest. Most Americans—including the majority of our church members, I fear—have been drinking deeply at the wells of modern individualism and autonomy. Opposed to any tradition, to any controls on theological thought, they see themselves as masters of their own souls, the champions of their own thought." (*Western Recorder,* September 1998)

Mohler's ideas about "controls on theological thought," reflected elsewhere in his ideas of "triaging" beliefs and setting parameters of doctrine, made an immediate impact on the seminary. He dismissed the dean of the school of social work and transferred the school to a nearby college. He asserted that Social Work did not belong in a theological seminary.

A number of local pastors with strong theological credentials were adjunct professors at the seminary. Several had manifested in one way or another dissatisfaction with the new direction of the SBC and a few related to some phase of the Cooperative Baptist Fellowship. Pastors of Broadway, St. Matthew's, Midlane Park, Beuchal Park, Clifton, Hurstborne, Third Avenue, and other Baptist churches were terminated as teachers at the seminary. Their sins amounted to failure to submit to the new regime or to have interest in the Cooperative Baptist Fellowship.

The trustees, amid much reaction within and without the school, decreed that the faculty must not disagree with the president in public. For Southern, with its history of disagreement on many issues and its sometimes rocky relationships between faculty and president, this was an unusual step.

Librarian Paul Debusman listened to a chapel address by SBC president Tom Eliff and thought a bit of the speech did not agree with the facts. He wrote a polite personal letter to Eliff explaining what he thought was the error. He said the letter was not belligerent but conciliatory. He closed his letter by saying that his "heart had been broken since 1979 by the way we had sniped at each other and I would to God that we could unite around the larger mission of sharing the gospel, discipling and equipping believers." The letter was promptly copied by Eliff to Mohler. A vice president "confronted Debusman in the librarian's office, demanded his keys and walked out, leaving the seminary treasurer to explain to Debusman he would receive one month's severance pay, which the seminary described as 'generous'. When Debusman returned to his office, it was locked. He had to secure administrative supervision while cleaning out files and belongings" (Paul D. Simmons, *Baptists Today*, May 1998). Debusman had been at Southern for 35 years. Due process guaranteed in civil law had no place at Southern Seminary.

Molly Marshall, a well known but sometimes controversial professor of theology, resigned her position. She indicated that she felt she was about to be terminated. She led a long line of teachers who sought other positions, retired, or read the *handwriting on the wall*. Several vacant faculty positions were filled quickly with persons who appeared to have little or no Southern Baptist background.

In 1996 the 93-year-old *Review and Expositor*, Southern's scholarly journal, broke its ties to the seminary. Joel Drinkard, a Southern professor and the journal's business manager, said:

> The editorial board announced it was reorganizing and that the publication should no longer be considered the faculty journal of Southern Seminary. Events over the past couple of years have made it obvious that the *Review and Expositor* cannot survive long-term in its historic relationship as the faculty journal of Southern Seminary....[Mohler was] shocked and saddened. (Baptists Today, April 1999)

These selected events illustrate the confusion and unhappiness existing at Southern during and after the "fundamentalist resurgence."

During this turmoil and a great deal more, enrollment plunged, support from alumni was seriously affected, and faculty morale was reported to be poor. After some years, enrollment began a slow climb, enhanced by numerous non-Southern Baptist students.

The faculty of today bears little resemblance to the previous ones. Present faculty seems to be comfortable with strong Calvinism and the apparent autocratic rule of the administration. The seminary has just launched a $70 million campus renovation. Moderate Baptists have begun efforts to form a new seminary in Kentucky.

## Southwestern Baptist Theological Seminary

Southwestern Seminary had a more tranquil history with fewer disturbances before the fundamentalist takeover. When the trustee board had a majority of fundamentalist sympathizers, the pace quickened. Tension with President Russell Dilday began almost immediately. His problem was that he was a thoroughgoing Baptist. Rumors had been circulating for many months that he would be terminated when a proper occasion appeared. When none appeared, on March 9, 1994 trustees dismissed Dilday as president, declaring they needed no reason since they had the votes. They locked his office, changed the access code to the computers and supervised the removal of his personal possessions.

The dismissal of this popular and very competent president shook the fundamentalist machine from coast to coast. Many denominational observers believe this event resulted in the election of Jim Henry as president of the SBC over the anointed favorite of the party, Fred Wolfe.

Dilday was popular in Texas and his dismissal became a catalyst for an ongoing review of the relationship between the independent state convention and the SBC. Many independent-minded Texans not only objected to the treatment of Dilday but also were dissatisfied with a great many other events in SBC life. The appointment of fundamentalist members to the various committees and boards angered the Texans. Many of the prominent moderate leaders were ignored in the selection of officials. Many of the faithful financial supporters of Baptist causes were left out of denominational activities. Churches with large gifts to the denomination were accused of having "liberal" pastors.

As the SBC leadership group narrowed to "those with us in the struggle" Texans grew more restive.

The seminary made every effort to put on a show that normalcy reigned. The work was not shattered as it was at Southern, but incidents continued, showing that at best the peace was an uneasy one. The board elected a woman teacher. Immediately objections were raised concerning a woman in authority over men—a constant problem for fundamentalists. The new "main-stream" president suggested that she was under the authority of the president on campus and her husband at home.

Southwestern's scholarly journal in 1996 prepared an issue examining *The Baptist Faith and Message*, the convention's confessional statement. Articles to be included were written by well-known Southern Baptist scholars such as William Hendricks, Molly Marshall, and Bill Leonard. When the writers became known, President Ken Hemphill canceled the issue "in the best interests of Southwestern and the Southern Baptist Convention." He said that these writers "do not stand for a strongly conservative view of *The Baptist Faith and Message*." (*ABP*, December 1996) This event was predictable. The fundamentalists could not tolerate the freedom of scholarly opinion expressed by these authors.

When the convention passed the addition to *The Baptist Faith and Message* concerning the submission of a wife to her husband, the seminaries were stuck with the confessional statement. After-the-fact acceptance of this new requirement was a source of concern to some. One Southwestern professor resigned rather than be bound by what were considered by many as unfair, unnecessary, and post-contractual requirements.

The position of Southwestern in Texas over the years as "our seminary" gave it special status as the state convention continued its distancing from the leadership of the SBC. When the fifth channel of giving allowing the exclusion of various SBC causes was presented, provision was made for the funding of Southwestern by the churches who so desired. The uneasy truce with the school continues. The true situation may be represented by the fact that Texas Baptists have already created two new seminaries at Baylor and Hardin-Simmons universities. They plan new initiatives for training laypersons and producing literature for their churches.

## Other Seminaries

Midwestern Seminary accelerated the retirement of its long-time president Milton Ferguson and elected ardent fundamentalist Mark Coppenger. After the usual period of turmoil about faculty and whether they were liberals, standards of evaluation were established. Calvinism was revisited and various declarations of orthodoxy were proclaimed. Interestingly, the status of women in the Kingdom occupied much attention within the trustees, the administration, and the faculty. According to the frequent press releases, the seminary established its position of compliance with the denominational wishes and in time seemed to get on with education.

Most recently, the trustees' executive committee met in executive session to consider the conduct of the president. Press reports reveal that the president was called on the carpet for "misappropriated anger" and his use of strong language—listed by one observer as PG—which was used toward too many associates and in informal settings. One such incident led to Coppenger's firing the chief academic officer, after which the trustees re-hired him the next day. According to ABP reports, the president was required to apologize and receive counseling for his anger. The reports state that these problems would make it difficult to function smoothly in the future. Coppenger commented that out of his repentance could come a great revival. Coppenger was later dismissed.

At Golden Gate Seminary, the usual financial problems continued to trouble the institution. The trustees abolished its emphasis on church music, secured the resignation of a few faculty members and promptly restored the program. When the convention adopted the statement on women as an addition to the confessional statement, a new problem arose for all the seminaries. Golden Gate trustees "approved several revisions to key governing documents that strengthen the institution's Southern Baptist identity. One such change to the seminary constitution affirms that the "cardinal beliefs on which the Golden Gate Baptist Theological Seminary is founded and in harmony with which it will operate are expressed in '*The Baptist Faith and Message*' approved by the Southern Baptist Convention...." Language was used that included any further changes made by the convention in *The Baptist Faith and Message*.

These changes included the change to the BFM on women. Golden Gate president William Crews told trustees:

> ...seminary faculty members also have 'indicated intention to continue their commitment' to the BFM. He said that came in response to his directive that any faculty member who could not abide by the current version of the statement should 'bring appropriate closure' to their service at Golden Gate Seminary. (*BP*, April 1999)

At New Orleans, the trustees elected the brother-in-law of Paige Patterson as its new president. To this point, there has been little posturing concerning the various events of SB life. The new president has led in the adoption of more than a half dozen new master of divinity degrees and proposes that graduating students be skilled in a dozen areas of expertise.

## New Controls

One of the most far-reaching changes in theological education in the Southern Baptist Convention is a new directive to the seminaries. All have been instructed to change their constitutions and/or bylaws to provide that the Southern Baptist Convention shall be "the sole member of the corporation," a legal step that places final authority in the Convention proper instead of the trustees. "Among other things, the action guarantees the SBC authority to determine the qualifications of trustees, elect and remove trustees and approve or override trustee actions" (*BP*, April 1999).

This rather innocuous-sounding legality actually introduces a new era of uncertainty and instability to an already disturbed system of education. Immediate alarm was registered by more than one school with the expressed fear that a single convention swept by the emotions of the moment could destabilize the entire system. The Executive Committee of the SBC, acting with questionable authority, is reported to have agreed that more than one convention vote would be required to dismiss trustees. For more than 100 years, the convention had successfully operated institutions without such a radical provision.

One of the more telling endorsements of these changes in Southern Baptist seminaries came from the convention's old nemesis, Jerry Falwell. In his *National Liberty Journal* Falwell wrote an article entitled "Southern Baptist Convention Defies Prophets of Doom." One of his principal points follows. "All six SBC seminaries now have fundamentalist presidents and faculties. All its agencies now have fundamentalist leadership." He added:

> We have also officially thrown our enthusiastic support behind the historic and unprecedented conservative 'revolution' which has taken place within the SBC during the past 20 years. Many of our sister churches have done the same and many more will in the months and years to come." (*Baptist Committed*, November 1998)

While all this was going on, many traditional Baptists, long supporters of the SBC, were saddened, alarmed, outraged, or all of the above. Theological education among Southern Baptists had been radically altered. Academic freedom existed now only within the strict confines of fundamentalist dogma or the whim of a president irritated by the actions of a professor. Great institutions were reduced to the rigid controls of the party line. Scholars with worldwide reputations were throttled or scattered to other places of service. Reputations were tarnished and careers shattered.

Reaction was not long in coming. New movements in theological education were born almost overnight. New seminaries or divinity schools were begun at the following institutions: Harden-Simmons, Baylor, Campbell, Gardner-Webb, Wake Forest, and Mercer Universities. A freestanding theological seminary was founded in Richmond. Special Baptist studies were initiated or enlarged at Duke, Emory, Texas Christian, and Vanderbilt.

## Which is The Baptist Way?

The late upheaval in Baptist life appears to be intellectually shallow and devoid of true theological underpinning. The supposed theology of "liberalism" has not been demonstrated. The takeover was based on half-truths using political methodology. There was a theological involvement, of course, but it was a call to a turn toward fundamentalist narrowness.

There is now a rush by theologians to give an explanation or in some cases an intellectual base to the movement. There is much discussion of postmodernism, individualism, interiorism, and personalism. The involvement of the rationalism of the enlightenment, deconstructionism, and paradigm shifts to new worldviews are all receiving attention.

Soul freedom, an historical landmark of traditional Baptists, has confronted a new array of accusations. That which the entire denomination frequently trumpeted now has been labeled with a spectacular series of "derogatory" descriptions. Liberty of conscience is labeled personalism, individualism, spiritual isolationism, antinomianism, anti-biblicalism, and deconstructionism. The priesthood of the believer is accused of allowing "anyone to believe anything." The accusations imply that any old-line Baptist who accepts this truth has abandoned the authority of Scripture or refuses the wisdom of the church.

The new mantra of the fundamentalist cause is "responsibility." One assumes, according to the so-called failures of the moderates to acknowledge Scripture, that responsibility is to the body politic with its "triaged parameters." If one surveys the steadily growing fence of theological and creedal strictures, the inevitable conclusion is that the responsibility is to the official interpretations and interpreters of the denomination.

One cannot escape the conclusions from denominational actions and pronouncements that the denomination must or has come up with a "triaged" theology with the "cocooned" vision of Scripture. The apparent alternative to this unbaptistic vision is that all other points of view subjects religious truth to "individual experience," which is the latest accusation against traditional Southern Baptists. This false dichotomy assumes that moderates have abandoned the authority of Scripture and the individual responsibility to God.

As the basic underlying sociological, theological, and educational grist is sorted out, it should be noted that the revolution was no cataclysmic contest over great intellectual goals. The revolution was about a recidivistic theology; the thrust for power and intent to dominate and control the flow of money into the largest evangelical body in the U. S. However, the implications went far beyond the intent of the revolutionaries.

## Colleges and Universities

The problems within the denomination and especially in the seminaries dropped incendiary bombs on a good Baptist system of higher education.

With the general direction of the SBC and many of the state Baptist bodies moving radically to the right colleges and universities owned by the states were threatened. If religious dogma could be set by a vote of a state convention, and it could, would the states follow the pattern of the national body? How much freedom to pursue the goals of education would be permitted? How would the periodic spasms of fundamentalist determinism affect the atmosphere of the academy? In the appointment of trustees, would the denominational politics determine the direction of the schools? Faculty selection, course offerings, administrative procedures, financial support, research grants, student applications, and the whole of academic life were involved in the direction of the denomination on a state level.

It appeared to many educational leaders that the schools were caught between volatile denominational fundamentalism and the legitimate demands of educational standards and principles.

The academy saw itself in search of truth wherever it led. No questions should be denied, no subject taboo, no opinion stifled, no predetermined answers dictated, and no external interference. Education is involved in endless investigation. Endless experiments or investigations of many disciplines are sure to provide some answers some religious leaders would reject. The very nature of higher education is threatened by "parameters" based on preconceived theological definitions. Not by the Bible, but by "cocoons of conclusions" about the Bible.

The denomination in the last two decades was declaring that it had found the truth. If the matter ended with religious conclusions, that was one thing. If extrapolations from that truth were imposed on the academy, that was another matter all together. Truth that was bound by the cocoon of fundamentalist parameters brought with it limits on the pursuit of knowledge, pointed out predetermined channels to knowledge, and insisted on non-scientific conclusions and questionable methodologies.

Of course, these problems had arisen before in most of the colleges and universities. Usually the schools were allowed to go on with education if they did not declare war on their constituencies. Uneasy peace reigned much of the time.

In the 1970s and 1980s, the religious power brokers had many questions for the academy.

Colleges feared a day when instructions were handed to them by religious leaders as to what was acceptable subject matter and investigative methodology. The fear of the substitution of religious dogma for free inquiry was a very real trauma for the schools. The faculties were as jealous of their academic freedom as was the preacher of his freedom in the pulpit.

It should be noted carefully that the vast majority of these schools had no desire to breach their relationships with the people who created and sustained them. Most of them had had few experiences with external dictation. Most faculties were Christian in their orientation and had no quarrel with the Bible though they often used their own vocabulary to describe their faith.

These faculties were no conglomeration of educated heathens bent on disproving Christian truth or subverting the faith of the students who came to them. In the main, they were and are Christians who found their ministry in the classroom. They usually supported and defended the state bodies that owned them and served the denominations in a wide variety of ways. Most were content to go about their calling and leave the politics of the denomination to others.

However, some of the college administrators had seen the cloud on the horizon. As the agitation within the national body in the 1970s and early 1980s grew to stormy proportions, some recognized the coming crisis. As early as 1983 one university president confided to me that he was preparing for a denominational divorce. In time, as the struggle intensified, others saw the need to do the same.

Many trustees and administrators saw the conflict as unavoidable, long-term, and devastating to the pursuit of their educational goals. Those who could began considering their intellectual and governance tools for possible flight. Charters, constitutions, and bylaws were studied with an intensity that probably never had been equaled.

The basic problems resided in whether boards of trustees could legally perpetuate themselves or the Baptist convention if the state controlled the election of trustees. In a few cases, it appeared that the school welcomed the opportunity to divorce itself from the control of the convention. In others, conscientious trustees and administrators saw no alternative. Nervous denominational executives found themselves again between forces they could not control. On the one hand was the increasingly demanding denominational leadership and on the other the perplexed and sometimes ambivalent college authorities.

Some found they were inextricably bound to the denomination with no legal way to declare independence. Some had no desire to separate themselves from their heritage. In other cases, the legal solutions were possible if not simple and independence was just a vote away. However, these actions always brought a denominational storm. It is probable that in most cases, the division brought great stress to both sides. Decades and in some cases more than a century of affiliation had fashioned a unique relationship between the churches and the schools. Divorce was a difficult and problematic solution to the denominational conflicts.

Within a few years, several of the denomination's best schools had formed self-perpetuating boards, declared their independence, and immediately promised fidelity to their founders. In almost every case, the school declared that it intended to maintain the same basic philosophical and religious traditions. They promised to stay as close to Baptists as possible.

In one way or another, the following institutions moved to self-control or to some modified method of electing boards of trust. Furman University, Wake Forest University, Mississippi College, Baylor University, Carson-Newman College, Hardin-Simmons University, Gardner-Webb University, and Samford University altered in some way their relationship to the sponsoring convention. Stetson and the University of Richmond had previously altered their relationships.

Inevitably, these moves created conflict with the sponsoring bodies. Some had funds withheld or withdrawn. Carson Newman College had funds escrowed by the Tennessee Convention for $2,229,389 for one year. The issue is pending.

As in the entire denomination, trust between colleagues suffered in the state bodies. Increased alienation between the various interests makes it extremely difficult to reach satisfactory solutions that properly recognize all concerns.

Several states lost fine institutions of higher learning. Of course, the denomination wonders how long or *if* the departing colleges will maintain standards that are acceptable. History of such moves by other Christian groups does not encourage Baptists.

There will be a general rethinking of the place of denominational schools in a world filled with social, economic, intellectual, and political fundamentalism.

The Baptist ideals of priesthood of the believer, soul freedom, and the free exercise of religion are assaulted on every side and their intellectual counterparts are feeling the heat.

# CHAPTER NINE

# NO FREEDOM FOR
# THE SOUL WITH A CREED

JAMES M. DUNN

Baptists are a
    funny breed,
A churchly crowd
    without a creed.
It is so.

A creed *prescribes* while a confession of faith *describes* one's approach to religion.

A creed is the necessary requirement to squeeze in and squeak by some theological gate.

We Baptists (the little "b" allows for kindred spirit among other churches) have no catechistic tests for believers. No acceptance of four or four hundred spiritual laws gets one right with God. Repentance and faith, a personal experience of God's grace—not intellectual assent to arguments—saves. It is a spiritual transaction. God's spirit is involved. We have no moral creed. Other, that is, than wonderful little maxims like these:

I don't drink, and I don't chew,
And I don't go with girls who do.

And:

Ain't nobody but Jesus gonna tell me what to believe.

Even believing and behaving according to code is not in itself redemptive. We "do right" because we *have been* saved not *to be* saved.

We certainly have no political creed. That is in large measure what produced the first Baptists by that name, a dogged dedication to religious freedom.

Non-creedalism drives some folks mad.

Always has. The apostle Paul had that problem with early Christians in Galatia. He called them stupid, senseless, foolish, idiots (various translations of Galatians 3:1). He reminded them that "it is precisely for freedom that Christ has set you free" (Galatians 5:1)—soul freedom backed up biblically.

Then in Galatians 5:12, he suggested radical surgery for the legalist who could not live without a rulebook religion. Then and now, rationalism reduces religion to rules. Those who clung to the past saw Paul as a no-law man, an antinomian. Their twentieth-century successors still libel with labels, striking out at those whom they do not understand.

A living faith is hard to take. It just literally drives some people crazy.

Creedlessness makes some true believers sad.

He said, "I just cannot believe a thing I cannot understand." Poor little fellow.

One's bucket of religion and spirituality is very small if it holds only what one "knows." In the mix of faith and reason, reason has a useful role. It explains or tries to, interprets, sells, and sometimes satisfies. However, if one's capacity for the divine dimension is limited by rational bounds, his or her pail is too small. There are tons of spiritual stuff none of us can get our puny minds around.

Whether limited by scientism like some liberals or by rational fundamentalism like some conservatives, the creed-chained character is pitiable.

A binding creed can turn pious people bad.

The philosopher Paschal said, "Men never do evil so fully, so happily, as when they do it for conscience's sake."

One need look at any day's lead news stories to see how hatred, hostility, and violence feed on religious fundamentalism. Other factors—economic, political, and cultural—are involved, but rigid religion makes people as mean as Tasmanian Devils out of otherwise decent disciples. Look at Israel, the Balkans, India, Northern Ireland, and on and on.

Who wants to fight and kill over propositions in the light of the amazing grace God offers?

A living faith not bound by creed makes Baptists glad.

It's love not law, faith not fact, persons not propositions, experience with God not expectations of persons at the heart of free and faithful Baptists and all believers of whatever brand.

In the blessed absence of a creed the confession of faith common to Baptists looms large: Jesus Christ is Lord.

That ancient confession is historically potent, theologically eclectic, spiritually significant, religiously accessible, biblically sound, and humanly available.

It is enough.

How can a creedless Christianity avoid "I-come-to-the-garden-alone" subjective religion? Doesn't faith without a rational checklist become nothing more than C. S. Lewis' "tickle around the gizzard"? Can a rope of sand bind together believers of the same bent?

Dangers abound. Soul freedom is a risky route. Experiment is close to the essence of experiential Christianity.

Yet, the risks are worth taking. The very meaning of "faith" is inextricably entangled in the Baptist brand of belief that insists upon an intimate individual religious commitment.

We stay under the umbrella of traditional Christianity. So far, at least, we Baptists have gotten by with this perilous practice of soul freedom with four substantial flying buttresses propping up the churches.

One is a radical Christ-centrism, the Christian doctrine, growing out of the radical monotheism that makes us such soul brothers and sisters with Jewish friends. That high and practical Christology takes seriously the words from 1 Timothy 2:5, "one mediator between God and all humankind." The same noble notion of an immanent and immediate friendship with Jesus sometimes slides into "WWJD" ethical temperature-taking. That's inadequate.

Then, there is, has been, is likely to be a reliance upon the Bible. Even a "liberal Baptist," an oxymoron, insists upon the authority of Scripture and argues that the written record of God's revelation is the "sole rule for faith and practice." The failure to buy the buzz word "inerrancy" hardly makes anyone a Bible-basher.

Another support for the centrality of soul freedom is the insistence on and acceptance of a regenerate church membership. If, indeed, one touts soul freedom for herself, she cannot escape granting it to all other born-again believers. This builds a fellowship of mutual respect, acceptance, and shared pilgrimage. Church members can support, empathize, even admonish and correct one another.

Finally, it must be admitted that one of the safeguards against utter subjectivism on the part of free souls has been the social system, the cultural props, the common-denominator identity that all Christians have in the civil-religion-shaped nation. A culture-wide comfort zone has shielded many believers of all stripes from hard questions and tough decisions about their personal faith. The day in which one could say, "Of course I'm a Christian—I'm an American, aren't I?" is gone.

The pluralism, multi-culturalism, and secularism (at its best and at its worst) that we know today requires us to rethink our deepest held beliefs. Soul freedom is certainly one of those beliefs for Baptists.

That soul freedom demands personal interaction and responsibility. Abstract propositions, however true or however close to The Truth, are not enough.

"I know whom I have believed." That's the Scripture (2 Timothy 1:12). Those are the words of the 1883 gospel song by Daniel W. Whittle, not "I know *what* I believe."

J. M. Dawson, first executive of the Baptist Joint Committee, once told me that he and George W. Truett consider themselves "Christian personalists." That terminology seems odd today, but the need for that brand of believer is great.

In fact, one cannot comprehend historic Baptists' passion for religious liberty without catching the intensely personal fever of their faith. It's not so much whether their beliefs are literal or liberal as that they are personal that counts.

The intensely personal nature of biblical faith is a Baptist birthmark. A University of Tennessee professor of philosophy and religious studies, Frank Louis Mauldin, is trying to help us catch on. He has written *The Classic Baptist Heritage of Personal Truth* (Providence House Publishers, 1999); "The Truth as It Is in Jesus" is the subtitle. The book contributes significantly to understanding Baptists and our hot-eyed, narrow-minded, loud-mouthed defense of religious liberty and her theological sister, soul freedom.

We have no book quite like this one. It examines and celebrates the biblical and the historic Baptist understanding of personal truth. We have books that explain Baptist faith and practice, others that consider Baptist history, and still more that examine a particular theological or denominational issue. But no other book undertakes the avowed fourfold purpose of (1) identifying and analyzing the distinctive notion of personal truth, (2) demonstrating the existence of a classic Baptist heritage of truth, (3) understanding what it means for Baptists in the classic heritage to equate truth with "the truth that is in Jesus," and (4) making the case that the story of personal truth (along with the stories of faith and freedom) constitutes the soul—the essential core and the common ground—of Baptist identity and integrity.

I heard a propositionalist testify: "I just cannot believe anything that I cannot understand." In this book Mauldin offers an antidote for that faith-threatening poison. The book and its biblical concept of incarnational truth also save us from the ditches on either side of the Christian way: *sola scriptura* on one side and *sola fide* on the other.

Mauldin documents and demonstrates that Baptists have always majored on experiential religion informed by the "Holy Word of God" and quickened by God's Spirit. The author says it all when he affirms that "Baptists...defend the thesis that truth is someone real, not something true." Jesus said, "I am the way, the truth and the life." One who reads this book may discover what a Baptist is.

Baptists are not alone in this dogged focus on personal faith. In 1972, Richard R. Niebuhr probed and provided a theoretical basis for belief, for affection rooted in religious experience. In the afterword of his book *Experiential Religion* he writes, "Human faith is not so much a sum of answers as it is a way of seeing and acting, and books about faith have first of all to describe what faithful men see and believe to be real."

Mauldin brings us one of those "books about faith" which does just that. John P. Newport in his foreword to the book calls it "a unique and important book." Newport acknowledges that Professor Mauldin's "emphasis on the fact that biblical truth is relational is very important."

In a current journal article Walter B. Shurden hits the same note, but denies that Baptist personalism is privatism or "Lone Ranger" religion. "To insist," says Shurden, "that saving faith is personal not impersonal, relational not ritualistic, direct not indirect, private not corporate has never meant for Baptists that the Christian life is a privatized disengagement from either the church or society." Even Walter Rauschenbush, father of the *Social Gospel*, gave 'experimental religion' as his first reason for being Baptist. Authentic faith requires soul freedom. One who has maneuvered and manipulated to mouth some counterfeit confession not profoundly personal is in danger of losing his immortal soul.

It's *who*, not *what*, we believe that makes us Christian.

CHAPTER TEN

# TRUTHS OR TRUTH—
# CREED OR SCRIPTURE

GRADY C. COTHEN

*Confessions*
*They constitute a consensus of opinion of some Baptist body....*
*We do not regard them as complete statements of our faith, having*
*any quality of finality or infallibility....*
*Any group of Baptists, large or small have the inherent right to draw*
*up for themselves and publish to the world a confession of their faith*
*whenever they may think it advisable to do so....*
*The sole authority for faith and practice among Baptists is the*
*Scriptures of the Old and New Testaments. Confessions are only guides in*
*interpretation, having no authority over the conscience.*
*They are statements of religious convictions, drawn from the*
*Scriptures, and are not to be used to hamper freedom of thought or inves-*
*tigation in other realms of life....*

*The Baptist Faith and Message, 1963*

"Not bossily telling others what to do but tenderly showing them the way...."
1 Peter 3:7 (The Message)

The serious differences between Baptists and the fundamentalists who claim
the distinction has gone on now for more than 20 years. In its formalized
beginning it was said to be about inerrancy of the Bible. It was in fact about
much more. Most writers on the history and meaning of the controversy have
recognized the inadequacy of simplistic explanations.

Either in an attempt to bolster an inadequate rationale or to give intellectual foundations to the arguments, the present day argument is said to be about objectivism and rationalism versus subjectivism and experientialism. The discussions use the language of philology or philosophy or theology and sometimes add confusion to the issues. It is clear that the argument has moved on from the restricted and simplistic insistence on inerrancy. That subject did not even qualify for serious analysis and discussion during the heat of the early days of the revolution. Many of its adherents were unaware of the many variations of the dogma. The discussion now is moving on to more meaningful analysis and intelligent inquiry.

Out of these developments several topics emerge from the more thoughtful and competent analysts:
• What is Truth?
• What is authority for a Baptist?
• Is the debate truly over objectivism and subjectivism?
• Does freedom in religion mean subjectivism?
• Does objectivism bind the truth of Scripture to its limitations?
• Can inerrantists logically settle for a propositional faith?

There are many more questions inherent in the basic argument between historic Baptist beliefs and fundamentalist dogma. Certain basic questions have to the present been neglected. One of them has been: What is truth? The question is a difficult one and requires many approaches to fathom its heart.

Frank Louis Mauldin has written a new book titled *The Classic Baptist Heritage of Personal Truth: The Truth as It Is in Jesus.* (Providence House Publishers, 1999). In it he insists that Baptists negated their seventeenth-century heritage and "did so by covering over personal truth with the impersonal and the propositional truths of reason, experience, doctrines, and facts." He makes the strong point that for Baptists:

> Truth is not a true belief, a true doctrine, or a true statement of any kind. Truth is not propositional. It does not arise from ways of knowing, out of epistemic starting-points and theories of knowledge or from a cognitive grasping of facts, ideas, experiences, judgments, or principles....Baptists rather defend the thesis that truth is someone real, not something true. It is someone encountered, not something known.

He postulates that truth is greater than truths and that there are not two kinds of truth. His categories of Baptist truth give us a fresh look at the Baptist heritage from the seventeenth century:

> Their (Baptists) categorical scheme consists of claims that (1) Truth is Jesus Christ, (2) truth is the Holy Trinity, (3) truth is the Holy Scriptures, (4) truth is abundant life and liberty, (5) truth is reasonableness...a truth that moves without violence, with a rational force in the reasonable soul enlightened by the Living God.

Mauldin, in one of the most heavily documented works I have seen in years, concludes that truth is not to be equated with subjective nor objective truths:

> Truth is not an abstraction drawn from either objective or subjective appearances...The dualism of subject and object, so indigenous to modern thought, has no place in the deep intimacy of the holy fellowship of faces, names, and stories in the gospel of grace found only in Jesus Christ...Classic Baptists know that an intimate fellowship with God depends solely upon God's gracious initiative. There is from the human side of the fellowship no way at all that leads to God, including that of a knowledge tied to universal, objective, or subjective truths.

Seeking truth as against truths would have been a good exercise during the two decades of controversy.

Mauldin traces the variations held by Particular and General Baptists. In his discussion of the problems of the Particular Baptists, he makes a comment that sounds strangely familiar:

> The age of Calvinistic scholasticism thus begins among Particular Baptists, and a strict orthodoxy of a decidedly rationalistic bent becomes the 'cardinal virtue of the churches'. Theological narrowness, spiritual aridity, abstruse debate, and rigid creedalism replace the zeal for the gospel so evident among earlier Particular Baptists, with the result that 'many poor sinners daily perish hereby for want of knowledge'.

Tragically, we have come out on the "post-modern" side with widely divergent understandings of the true nature of truth. Much of the argument has not been about a true Baptist heritage but about "who is going to run this show." Those who were the better politicians won that point and have run the show into a non-Baptistic cul-de-sac.

It is unfortunate that the problems were discussed in a context that skirted issues crucial to being a Baptist. Walter Shurden summarized the argument succinctly:

> Fundamentalists argued for stricter controls in light of what they believed was too much freedom that had issued in false teachings. Moderates, on the other hand, lobbied for freedom in the face of what they thought was a non-Baptistic and paralyzing control. This central issue may also be described as 'conformity versus liberty' or 'uniformity versus diversity.' Fundamentalists were interested in theological conformity and denominational uniformity. Moderates were interested in liberty of conscience and denominational diversity. (*Not a Silent People*)

In time, fundamentalism bound its message of truth to a series of statements about the Bible and some moral issues derived from the Bible. The result sounded strangely like the problems of the Particular Baptists, and the renewed emphasis on Calvinism did not help the situation. Traditional Baptist hostility to creedal "cocoons" began at least in the seventeenth century and was renewed by the first meeting of the Southern Baptist Convention.

The brethren gathered in 1845 declared, "We have constructed for our basis no new creed."

They were doubtless familiar with the Philadelphia Confession on which John Leland a half-century earlier commented at some length. His conclusion bears on the present discussions:

> Confessions of faith often check any further pursuit after truth, confine the mind into a particular way of reasoning, and give rise to frequent separations....It is sometimes said that heretics are always averse to confessions of faith. I wish I could say as much of tyrants.

He was not decrying the truths often contained in confessions, but was commenting on their limitations.

While in the realm of history and the search for reality, another statement by Robison James is relevant to the present discussions stuck on subjectivity and objectivity. In *Beyond the Impasse,* James says:

> Neither our propositional formulation of doctrinal truth nor our subjective religious experience is absolute. Both of these things are relativised by being included within a 'third', namely the mothering reality in which the first two inhere, the biblical story in which the living, acting, speaking God relates to us ongoingly.

Once again we ask, what is authority for a Baptist?

Within the last two decades, the philosophical and theological emphasis of the largest of Baptist groups has changed significantly. This is not to say that many of the doctrinal positions of the SBC are not biblical. It is to say that the statements about the Bible and the interpretations that have been "officialized" on various issues have been substituted for a more dynamic understanding of biblical truth.

The creedalism of the SBC has been a creeping and potentially deadly disease. Most churches and the saints seem to have no idea of the nature of the changes. There are several points that need attention.

First, the creedal problems begin with *The Baptist Faith and Message*. Almost all Southern Baptists would agree with the basic doctrinal statements including the oft-debated statement about the Bible. There are several problems, however. The confession has become the basis of fellowship. It has often been interpreted by various meetings of different groups and those interpretations have been equated with the will of Southern Baptists. This problem includes the report of the Peace Committee to the SBC.

Instructions were issued in 1969 to the seminaries and agencies of the denomination that the document (*BFM*) is to be used to "teach and write in keeping with and not contrary to." The interpretations of the document reported by the Peace Committee imposed more stringent controls on the agencies and seminaries. The recent addition of the article related to the family raises serious questions as to the wisdom of such post-contract (with faculty and officials) use of such a document.

The addition of the interpretations of the Peace Committee to the body of directions to the institutions of the SBC is a matter of utmost importance. While they have been discussed in another context, they are significant to this discussion. The convention in approving the report and making it the law of the body instructed all that (1) they were to accept a literal interpretation of the creation story; (2) they were to accept the usual attributions of authorship to biblical books; (3) all miracles described in Scripture did occur as supernatural events in history; and (4) the historical narratives are accurate and reliable.

The committee offered no rationale for these conclusions, which they insisted that most Southern Baptists believe. An actual survey conducted by the denomination showed some interesting results. The respondents were asked to select from five statements the one that describes their feelings about the Bible. Thirty five percent chose "The Bible is the actual word of God, and is to be taken literally word for word." Forty nine percent chose, "The Bible is the inspired word of God. It contains no errors, but some verses are to be taken symbolically rather than literally." Eleven percent chose "The Bible is the inspired word of God, but it may contain historical and scientific errors" (*Baptist Courier*, May 1991).

Second, the convention has adopted a growing list of motions and resolutions and has entertained unofficial discussions that are interpreted by some as the instructions of the SBC to institutions, state bodies, and churches. Resolutions and/or motions related to the priesthood of the believer, the pastor as the ruler of the church, the place of women in ministry and in the family, and homosexuality and abortion all impinge on the decisions of the faithful.

Before 1979, convention resolutions had no formal status as far as the various institutions were concerned. Now they were to be taken literally as instructions to the agencies. One seminary faculty member was urged to resign before termination proceedings because she had not paid proper attention to "an action of the convention." Resolutions and motions that are passed by the national body are now viewed as the sense of the convention and have immediate and sometimes precipitous results in the institutions. Actions on the status of women, the problems of homosexuality, and the matter of abortion have all had serious effects on the state conventions, the associations, and local churches.

Third, the concentration of power in the Executive Committee has created a hierarchical problem that causes tremors through the whole of the denomination. The practical control of the budget, which has funneled new money to the Committee and its political-ethics committee and the seminaries instead of the promised plan of funding missions, is causing great concern. The total control of the Baptist Foundation, the increased influence over the seminaries, and the almost total acceptance of its reports by the convention make the Executive Committee's opinions highly controlling.

Fourth, the assumption that the votes of the Executive Committee and the Convention are determinative for the denomination is a serious shift toward creedalism. An example is the action of the Convention excluding certain churches for their attitude toward homosexuality. Immediately some states and associations moved toward the same action. The position of the national body on women in ministry has encouraged action by local associations to follow suit.

Fifth, the flight to creedalism has been largely based on propositional definitions of truth. This is not to say that all such postulations are in error. It is to say that the rule of faith and practice has moved from Holy Scripture to words about Scripture and individual interpretations of words about

Scripture. The confession of faith, while probably acceptable to most Baptists, is about Scripture; but when it becomes the reference point instead of Scripture, it is being improperly used. It is a return to the Reformation, which substituted rationalism for the Bible. This by "inerrantists."

All this despite the fact that *The Baptist Faith and Message* statement clearly says "that sole authority for faith and practice among Baptists is the Scriptures of the Old and New Testaments. Confessions are only guides in interpretation, having no authority over the conscience."

Sixth, the easy "believeism" that demands rational assent to theological propositions threatens the beginning of Christian experience and its dynamic relationship to Christ, His Lordship, and the believer's discipleship. Salvation does not begin with the intellectual acceptance of theological dogma. It is a personal encounter with the Christ, the person's sin, unconditional surrender, and the beginning of life-long discipleship.

Any system of truth that fails to issue in personal relationship to God through Jesus Christ is not Christian truth.

Seventh, there is a tendency to add constantly to the list of requirements for a person to qualify as a "good Baptist." These criteria for "good Baptists" are being woven into the fabric of state conventions, associations, and churches.

Eighth, the factor of intimidation of pastors, churches, associations, and even state bodies is seriously underestimated. With national leadership moving in new directions and a pastor's future in the denomination dependent on the goodwill of the brethren, the results are potentially very hazardous. A serious criterion of the fundamentalist leadership for recommendation of a pastor to a church is the question, "Was he with us in the struggle?" Since such leadership controls the convention agencies, seminaries, mission boards, and many of the state organizations, a pastor "not with us" is in a precarious position. He has no potential for leadership in the denomination and is not recommended to most churches.

## Is the SBC Moving Toward Creedalism?

A short look at the emphases of the denomination in the last two decades will illustrate the problems. The following items have occupied the attention of the denomination for extended periods. Each has been proclaimed essential or desirable to being a good Baptist. These seem to be the "irreducible minimums" long desired by some of the leadership:

- The 1963 *Baptist Faith and Message* with its pages of doctrinal statements
- The 1969 requirement that employees shall teach and write in keeping with and not contrary to the BFM
- The concept of inerrancy of original manuscripts—words about the Bible
- The Glorieta statement of the seminary presidents
- The Peace Committee report with instructions that agencies form their professional staffs according to the interpretation of the committee of what Southern Baptists believe
- Doctrinal positions advocated by the convention on such issues as women in ministry, homosexuality, abortion, priesthood of believer, and pastoral authority
- The Chicago Statement on Inerrancy with its dozen qualifications about the Bible
- "Triage of doctrinal positions to determine order of importance"
- Stipulation that no Baptist who is a member of a church of which the pastor is involved with the Cooperative Baptist Fellowship may write for denominational publications or serve on any national committee or board (and in some state conventions)
- Doctrinal parameters, many yet unspecified
- What seems to be another list that may be called the "essentials of orthodoxy," some enunciated by leaders who act as if they are enfranchised to declare dogma
- Social and political issues such as necessity of school prayer; vouchers for students in religious schools; display of religious objects in public places; religious observance in public functions; promotion of private and home schools; and participation in political campaigns to control school boards, congress, and other governmental functions as well as impeachment of the president (Some of these are positions staked out by the Ethics Commission but apparently have become the official position of the denomination.)

Ecumenical oddities continue, such as cooperation with Catholics, Jews, Church of Christ, many evangelical groups including Pentecostals, and any others who support a given issue. Yet, the denomination refuses to accept any funds contributed to missions or educational causes that come through the Cooperative Baptist Fellowship. These are Baptists who built the denomination fundamentalists are taking credit for building.

Whatever else may be said of creedalism in the SBC, the general methods of operation are radically different today from those twenty years ago. The claim is made that the denomination has been restored to its traditional position; yet, at no point in history has the denomination resembled what it is today. The differences from its historical positions are such that it would not be recognizable to its founding fathers.

All this sounds sterile, arid, and rational. Quoted below is one of an almost infinite number of such results of all this. The title is "No Longer a Writer," written by Margaret Caldwell of Virginia and first published in the *Religious Herald*:

> I have been expecting this day for quite a while. Yet, foresight is meager comfort against a resurgence of grief, personal anger and sadness for the Southern Baptist Convention.
>
> Today I spoke with my long-time friend and editor at LifeWay Christian Resources (formerly Baptist Sunday School Board). I asked if she planned to use me as a special education curriculum writer again this year. She asked me, *as she is now required to do* [emphasis mine], whether I belonged to a church affiliated with the Cooperative Baptist fellowship, in which the pastor is actively involved. I knew where that question was leading. The 'litmus test' continues to trickle down.
>
> "Yes," I replied to my editor, as tears filled my eyes. If a label were applied to me, I would be tagged a theological moderate-conservative, professing, active Baptist Christian. I am a member of a church whose central question is, 'What does God want us to do?'
>
> It is a congregation whose members give support to the Southern Baptist Convention, The Cooperative Baptist Fellowship, (and state convention and association).
>
> My friend was apologetic as she explained that I could no longer write curriculum for Southern Baptists. I do not blame my editor; this is not her doing. I expressed anger at the effects of narrow-minded fundamentalists' policies, and sadness. My hurt is very small, when compared with that of denominational leaders who have suffered much. I know others who have lost places of services and jobs....
>
> The irony is that I wrote on a 2.5 grade level, simply telling the Bible story...I challenge any fundamentalist, moderate or liberal to find anything in my...writing with which they would disagree....Of course, my friends with retardation do not care about theological political correctness. It only matters that I love them and share Christ.

Multiply this story by many hundreds, perhaps thousands, and then decide about creedalism.

CHAPTER ELEVEN

# DON'T VOUCH FOR VOUCHERS

## JAMES M. DUNN

Soul freedom, for all its theological roots and implications, has become an article of faith for the American way.

The separation of church and state is more than a convenient arrangement. It is the rock-bottom presupposition about the right and proper relationship of basic institutions.

There is in this land a general, universal assumption that no person is better or more important than anyone else. That spawns the ultimate democratic entitlements for all and these entitlements include a decent basic education.

Along come rich folks and racists, elitists and greedy senior citizens, frightened parents and profiteers, retreating religionists and institutionalists desperate to save their failing schools. With them are political opportunists and public institution pessimists, privatization pushers and right-wing philosophers who never thought kindly of democracy in the first place. All these "true believers" have sold many Americans a bill of goods. They have created lots of misled and misinformed voters who think that "school choice" or "vouchers" are the answer.

Yet, a populist and pious, democratic and devout, good citizen and good Christian reliance on soul freedom informs a different perspective on vouchers. If one genuinely seeks soul freedom for everyone, he can't vouch for vouchers.

Two news stories on the front page of the March 4, 1999 *New York Times* help define the dilemma facing public education.

One headline reads: "School Chief Drawing a Line Over Vouchers." New York City Schools Chancellor Rudy Crew warned Mayor Rudy Giuliani that he would resign if the mayor pushes through a voucher program to spend tax dollars for children to attend private schools. A person close to Crew said, "He feels that it is the beginning of the end of public education, period, if you start funneling taxpayer dollars into private education."

The other headline reads: "Court Says Schools Must Pay for Needs of Disabled Pupils." The U.S. Supreme Court ruled that public schools must pay all nonmedical costs for disabled students. The specific decision requires Cedar Rapids, Iowa schools to provide continuous one-on-one, in-school support for a 16-year-old quadriplegic. The Individuals with Disabilities Education Act guarantees a "*free appropriate public education* to students with disabilities" (emphasis added).

The headlines touch on the tough choices we all face regarding public schools. The high court sustained the idealistic goals of common schools for all. Years of historical experience stand behind the all-American conviction. Jefferson said, "If a nation expects to be ignorant and free, in a state of civilization, it expects what never was and never will be."

Over the years we have as a people spelled out those ideals to mean that it is the responsibility of all of us to teach the disabled, the difficult to discipline, the distant child not near a school, the disturbed young person, and any other child. "School choice" is well named because the nonpublic school makes the choice. Rudy Crew is right. Voucher schemes would begin the end of public education. Some people want that. Some Baptist leaders of the fundamentalist stripe are endorsing a movement to take all Christian children out of the public schools.

Most voucher advocates, however, have simply been misled, have not thought it through, or perhaps are thinking too anecdotally.

Earlier this century, some folks in Europe ignored grand schemes because the trains ran on time. Their personal lives were easier. They self-centeredly missed the big picture.

One's heart goes out to all those who have bought the limited vision of voucher propagandists: "it's about competition"; "the public schools have failed"; "it's your money to spend as you see fit"; "public education won't suffer."

It's not politically correct, nor is it sweet and gentle, to name the demons that drive the push for vouchers. Yet, those darker dimensions can be characterized as follows.

*Political*: Appeals to cynicism and hopelessness, the worst aspects of our nature. Some have bought the big lie that "public schools have failed."

*Selfish*: "I only want what's best for my child." Exactly. Shortsighted sacrifice of the long-term public good for immediate personal satisfaction.

*Parochial*: I mean "restricted to a narrow scope." "Hoss blinds" keep some from seeing beyond their own little corner.

*Greedy*: Prophets of economic justice have always been accused of fomenting class hatred, dividing the rich from the poor. Remember Amos, chapter 4, when the eighth-century prophet took on the "fat cows of Bashan" and James, chapter 5, when the earthly brother of Jesus said, "Howl and weep you rich." "Rich"—a category into which most well-to-do Americans fall. Biblical justice demands special treatment of the poor.

*Racist*: I recently heard a lovely-looking and sophisticatedly socialized South Carolina lady lament what has happened "since we let 'them' into ouah schools." I have not yet met a "Yankee" who understands the hate and fear that fuel the fanatical push for segregated academies. That push is a major force for voucherizing education.

*Shortsighted*: There is always a temptation to sacrifice the permanent on the altar of the temporary.

Please, please, don't get defensive. I know all these awful adjectives don't apply to you. I understand earnest, honest people of good will differ. It's true that there is vast ignorance and much misunderstanding on both sides of the debate.

However, if public education is broke, let's fix it. Every child is entitled to a free, quality public school.

"School choice" is the right name for a wrongheaded reform of public education. It is the private schools with the choice—they decide whether to accept a child or not.

I cannot vouch for vouchers. Such schemes are at least:

*Unpredictable*: Running the risk of funding even Nazi, Ku Klux Klan ventures or worse;

*Unfair*: Giving social sanction to schools that can reject the discipline problem, the deficient learner, the disabled, while public schools serve all children;

*Unconstitutional*: Violating the no establishment clause of the First Amendment since the courts have made it clear that it is illegal to launder funds for faith-based schools by filtering them through parents;

*Unworthy*: Blessing the secession of the successful from their social responsibility by providing welfare for the well-off (Nothing could be much more regressive.);

*Unthrifty*: Starting a new federal spending program with a multi-billion-dollar expenditure, highlighting the hypocrisy of precisely the politicians who are so concerned with the deficit;

*Undemocratic*: Exempting elitist schools from public control, beyond the reach of the voter, unaccountable to the local electorate;

*Unjust*: Devising a discriminatory *de facto* windfall for the larger in-place parochial system, which belongs to one church;

*Unethical*: Destroying the public school system by siphoning off money, skimming strong students, and draining parent power from public education, leaving two separate and unequal systems—private and pauper;

*Unprincipled*: Subscribing to an odd principle of equity: "Since I've decided to send my child to a special school, you—all taxpayers—must subsidize me."

*Uncalled-for*: Ignoring voters who have turned down 16 of 17 tuition tax credit or voucher plans in state referenda and the 60 percent to 30 percent rejection of vouchers by the American people (Peter D. Hart survey, 1995);

*Uneconomical*: Inventing a new escalatory entitlement while slashing federal aid to public education from a high of 9 percent of the budget in 1949 to a proposed 1.4 percent in 1999;

*Unsuccessful*: Pretending that the Wisconsin experiment is a winner, though it has failed economically, educationally and politically;

*Unsympathetic to freedom*: Inviting the inevitable government entanglement with regulations and guidelines that always follow public monies (He who pays the fiddler still calls the tune.);

*Unworkable*: Recognizing that there has not yet been a plan proposed that would cover tuition and transportation for the poorest children;

*Untruthful*: Shifting money from one pocket to another to claim that public funds would not benefit the sponsoring church or advance sectarian purposes (A tad shady, eh?);

*Unsustainable*: Raising false hopes among poor people who will never with any such scheme be able to send their children to exclusive schools;

*Un-American*: Establishing a new sort of taxation without representation on the controlling boards of publicly funded private schools;

*Unfaithful*: Failing the biblical call for believers to be salt and light in the world, witnesses in the public square;

*Un-Christian*: Accusing those of us who don't want our tax dollars to bankroll private causes of discriminating against Christians. Shame!

Other than all that, vouchers might be O.K.

There are choices we can make about school:

*Either* welcome all sorts of charter and choicy schools from those of Heaven's Gate to Hell's Angels,
*Or* allow government to determine which religions are worthy and which ones are unworthy, *religio licita* or *religio illicita*.

*Either* require chosen schools to play by the rules that all public schools must follow, providing for disabled, distant, and discipline-problem children—all children,
*Or* stop talking about "competition" when there is no level playing field in the education game and when there are different rules for different teams.

*Either* demand total freedom for the faith-based school to evangelize, proselytize and remake kids in its own image, however sectarian,
*Or* without whimpering, accept in our church-related schools the reporting, monitoring, entanglement, snooping, and meddling that must always follow government funding.

*Either* throw enough money into vouchers for the lowliest kids to have access to the topmost schools,
*Or* admit that the pilot projects and experiments are actually a wedge to afford another middle class entitlement.

*Either* embrace the view of 86 percent of Americans that "a good public school education" is one's "right as a citizen," not a "privilege to be earned," *Or* proceed to rob the public schools of parental support, dollars, and other resources, setting up separate and unequal school systems and institutionalizing injustice.

*Either* accept anecdotes about "how well little Billy's doing in a parochial school," *Or* find antidotes for the poison of self-serving escapism from social responsibility to the common school.

*Either* perpetuate the fiction that without actual tax dollars (same serial numbers?) used to teach religion, there's no church-state violation, *Or* confess that the influx of voucherized tax monies into church schools frees up funds for the pervasively sectarian mission of those schools, as simple and unethical as moving money from one pocket to another.

*Either* assume vouchers are rightly-claimed tax rebates for parents to spend on any educational venture, *Or* tell the truth that taxes taken from the public treasury are merely money laundered for non-public institutions (it's still unlawful to do indirectly what cannot be done directly).

*Either* assume that the courts can finally settle the matter, *Or* insist that everything declared legal by a court (even the Supreme Court) is not, therefore, automatically right or good or moral or ethical or fair or just.

*Either* go along with those who want no separation of church and state, *Or* agree with James Madison, who said, "Religion and Government will both exist in greater purity, the less they are mixed together."

We have choices. I'm with President John F. Kennedy when he said, "I believe in America where the separation of church and state is absolute... where no church or church-related school is granted any public funds or political preference."

Soul freedom is safeguarded by not allowing government at any level to fund religious institutions.

How about you?

# CHAPTER TWELVE

# THE GOSPEL— PERCEPTION AND REALITY

## GRADY C. COTHEN

*Religious Liberty*
*...Church and state should be separate. The state owes to every church*
*protection and full freedom in the pursuit of its spiritual ends. In provid-*
*ing for such freedom, no ecclesiastical group or denomination should be*
*favored by state more than others....The church should not resort to the*
*civil power to carry on its work. The gospel of Christ contemplates spiri-*
*tual means alone for the pursuit of its ends. The state has no right to*
*impose penalties for religious opinions of any kind. The state has no right*
*to impose taxes for the support of any form of religion.*

*The Baptist Faith and Message, 1963*

"...you bring disrepute on the Gospel." 2 Peter 2:2

This one comes back to haunt me.

She stood on the church steps warmed in the words of the pastor. "God loves you and so do we." The baby in her womb stirred and terror swept over her again. Her hurt and confusion were like bile in her throat. Her uncle had threatened to kill her if she told of the rape. Her mother had cried all night the night before. Her father would not talk to her and her brother said, "how could you, didn't you ever hear of birth control?"

Despairing, confused, alone and alienated, what should she do? Her options were limited: abortion was the easiest, the quickest, perhaps had fewer long-term problems. Bear the child amid the family's anger and embarrassment and put it up for adoption. Bear the child and keep it—and stigmatize herself for life and probably never be able to have a normal family. Such a child would have a tough time in her family and maybe in school. The child would not know the warmth of an extended family—grandparents, cousins, family gatherings. The father was afraid of being exposed and would not provide for the child; and besides, he was long gone.

And—she thought he had given her AIDS.

Would the child be born with the disease? The chances were high.

Abortion!

But when she went to the clinic to talk about it, the crowd now restrained by ropes screamed at her and the nurse who opened the door. She knew that doctors had been shot for performing the operation. She was terrified and humiliated.

"God loves you and so do we!" Where was "we"? Some who yelled the loudest were members of her church.

Where were God and "we"?

She was a Baptist and had heard of God's love all her life. Does God just love you when everything is okay? Why were all these people yelling at her if they loved her? Something was wrong but she was too confused to diagnose the problem. What was real?

Baptists were for over a hundred years somewhat different from other "mainline denominations." They were theologically conservative. They were hesitant to embrace the latest theological fad or debate the issue of the day. Across a half-century they had been growing spiritually on such matters as racial justice. Social and ethical issues became more important as the group faced a dynamic and tumultuous world. The world saw them as a backward (by the standards of others) people who were slow to change. Sometimes their profession of biblical faith and practice of it were too far apart for comfort of the conscience.

Yet, even if they had the heavenly treasure in pots of clay, they were called Bible believers. They were "faith in Christ" people. Often others said they were behind the times but they clung to faith in "beyond the times." En masse they were not very concerned with the critics while individually they sometimes cringed at the derision and compromised.

They were by the standards of other Christians evangelistic and missions work was the hallmark of their sometimes-feeble efforts. They talked about these things more than they did them, but despite their doublespeak they became America's largest evangelical body. They appointed and supported the world's largest evangelical body of missionaries.

They founded an effective and recognized group of theological seminaries—all theologically conservative though this was questioned by the fundamentalists. More than 50 colleges and universities were founded and operational. A number of these schools achieved national recognition as excellent private schools. Theological education was virtually free for students for a 100 years and the other schools were economical by private standards.

Despite its growing ethical and social concerns, these Baptists believed that society would be changed by changing individuals. Righteousness rose from the people's relationship with God and did not come down from government enforcement of rules and regulations. They were possessed of the strange idea that organized religion should not be mixed with organized government. They were accused of not being interested in social problems and for years did seem to ignore far too many of them. They could not accept government money for faith projects since public policy always follows public money. If they accepted tax money for religious purposes, they could soon expect to have government agencies checking on the use and stewardship of that money.

Then the fundamentalists took control of the Southern Baptist part of the Baptist family. They changed their Baptist spots to become extensively involved with politics. Cunning politicians welcomed the intrusion of these new religious allies.

Both the politicians and the fundamentalist Baptists knew they would gain support for their agenda by joining forces. Strangely, the agendas were remarkably similar, especially as segments of the Republican Party became influenced by the religious right wing. The religious right as a political entity came into sharp focus and weighed in on moral, ethical, and religious issues.

These groups proclaimed their moral superiority and organized to legislate and intimidate the opposition. Religious rightists believed that at least part of their agenda could be legislated and morality enforced by law. Abortion, homosexuality, and violence in the entertainment and media worlds all became items in the struggle for power. For a number of years, the Moral Majority and the Christian Coalition claimed the blessings of conservative and fundamentalist Christians, and together with the politicians they wielded considerable power. An almost unlimited number of conservative organizations joined these efforts.

It is not incidental that concerns outside the U. S. closely parallel some of those at home. In his article, referred to earlier, William Martin calls attention to the fact the Egyptians are concerned with "the religious card" used with "startling frequency" in the U. S. government. The Chinese express anxiety at the interference in their affairs in the name of religion. One representative of the Middle East Council of Churches in Beirut complained that American religious activity brings back "memories of the Crusades" and decries what to them appear efforts to evangelize Muslims (*Foreign Policy*, Spring 1999). Such activity with Muslims is normally done by Christians since Muslims in turn attempt to evagnelize Christians. As an appearance of foreign policy, it is altogether a different matter.

After the overthrow in the Southern Baptist Convention, the leadership brought to the struggle their brand of fundamentalism. The new leadership of the Ethics Commission openly avowed the idea of legislating morality. One of the key methods of control was the exclusion and denunciation of all fellow believers who did not subscribe to this brand of activism.

Contrary to its history, the denomination began for years to solve social, ethical, and moral problems by organized utilization of political power. Lobbying, arm-twisting, organizing, and other political methods became the order of the day.

Of crucial importance to the perception of unbelievers was the unending condemnation of those who practiced abortion and homosexuality as well as of the entertainment industry. The belligerence of Christian ministers, churches, and other religious organizations in these denunciations was often surprising and offensive to outsiders.

The organized efforts to close clinics, the violence that resulted from these efforts, the inflamed rhetoric on a dozen subjects, and the intimidation of those who disagreed raised in the public mind important questions: Is all this Christian? Is this what Christ taught? Do these attitudes represent the church? Are the methods of the politician used by religious bodies baptized by God? Are these people giving us what the Bible teaches? Do they hate sinners as much as they seem to? Must we all submit to the extremes they seem to dictate? What right do these people have to control the conduct of the rest of society? What is religion doing trying to control civil government? How far will government go in yielding to the demands of the Religious Right?

The new Southern Baptists leadership brought a number of issues to the conflict that seriously colored the reaction of the public to evangelical faith. In their annual conventions they passed a number of resolutions that received international attention. One resolution was used as joke material by late-night comedians. The convention passed a resolution that said to the public that *wives must be submissive to their husbands*. Even to Bible-honoring

THE GOSPEL—PERCEPTION AND REALITY 109

conservatives the resolution seemed to omit Paul's additional admonition to the husbands to love their wives. They ignored the context of the quoted scripture.

Another series of actions related to women in ministry. Some Baptist churches had ordained women deacons for more that 100 years. As women sought to enter the professional ministry, the reactions of the fundamentalists were immediate and vociferous. A number of local associations voted to withdraw fellowship from churches with women deacons. Any church ordaining a woman to the ministry was subject to exclusion by the local association or the state body. All this was comparatively new and created frequent conflicts. A couple of years before the resolution on submissive wives the body had passed a resolution asking all the faithful to boycott the Walt Disney Company because the type of entertainment being produced was not considered family material. Other groups joined this effort. Few of them knew that Disney had more than 200 business enterprises. The convention voted to have their annual meeting in Orlando in 2000, asking their members to avoid the Disney facilities.

In another meeting, the convention passed a motion to make a special effort to target and evangelize the Jews. Given the history of the organization, this was a rather ordinary expression of interest to some messengers. This type of expressed concern about the spiritual condition of others was not unusual for Baptists. The problem, however, was that the group who brought the resolution drew so much attention to itself that everything it did attracted interest. This problem brought about immediate and vigorous reaction not only from Jews but from many others. The reaction in South Florida was spontaneous and sometimes volatile. Many friendly discussions between Christians and Jews were disturbed or terminated.

The denomination, while seeking relationships with other evangelical denominations, effectively excluded all Southern Baptists who related in any way to the Cooperative Baptist Fellowship. False accusations were made that the CBF approved of abortion and homosexuality. The fundamentalists were horrified at the prospect that women could be ministers. Further, the CBF was considered to be in competition with the SBC. The theological differences of the two groups had been acceptably compatible for 150 years. However, the new SBC leadership could fellowship with groups with very different beliefs, such as Catholics and Pentecostals, while condemning and casting out their spiritual brothers and sisters for imaginary or minor differences.

To further alienate the general public, after the aborted effort to remove President Clinton from office, the denomination's leadership continued its divisive commentary. SBC president Paige Patterson said that the Senate's decision not to convict the president of impeachable offenses has "sown the seeds" for the demise of the country! Southern Seminary president Al Mohler said: "Confronted with one of the greatest moral challenges in its history, the Senate responded with moral apathy." Richard Land of the Ethics Commission commented that the "most appropriate word for this whole process from beginning to end is 'pathetic.'"

Comments on Washington politics by the fundamentalist leadership of the SBC sounded strikingly similar to their Republican cohorts. The divisive issue sounded much more like politics as usual than a great moral crusade. In no way, however, does this justify the conduct of the president.

Ironically, this event occurred during the time SBC leader Richard Land (and perhaps others) attended a meeting to discuss civility in public life. Land is quoted as saying that it is important to remain civil in these discussions and to *"disagree on issues without being disagreeable."* He also quoted Martin Luther King, who said: "Those whom you must change, you must first love."

In this general connection, the president of the SBC at its meeting in June 1999 called on the Immanuel Baptist Church of Little Rock to discipline its most famous member, President Bill Clinton. Baptists have never taken kindly to outsiders interfering in the business of the local church. To intensify the problem two motions were made from the floor of the annual convention meeting, asking the church to exercise "discipline" of the wayward president.

Alongside this series of events the latest prominent addition to the Baptist fold, Jerry Falwell, produced his latest observation. Falwell took a shot at the popular English children's program, "The Teletubbies." One of the elves wore purple and had a triangle on his head. Falwell said the purple represents the gay pride color, while the triangle is the gay pride symbol. Falwell surmised publicly that Tinky Winky is a homosexual. Even *Miami Herald* columnist Leonard Pitts thought this was a proper subject for extended ridicule of the Falwell. Again the new Baptist leadership provided several weeks of material for the late-night comedians. The cause of civic morality suffered another blow.

## The Slaughter of the Innocents

One of the most far-reaching and devastating series of events in Baptist history occurred when the fundamentalists gained a voting majority in the SBC. All told more than 200 professionals, including senior executives, faculty, and management, were summarily dismissed and required to retire or find other work. Almost none had a genuine hearing or opportunity to provide a defense. Almost none had any charges brought against them. A few were called "liberals" but no trials or substantive evidence was revealed. There were no assertions of malfeasance, immoral conduct, or incompetence. Their careers abruptly ended because they were in office when the fundamentalists seized power.

At the Sunday School Board, about 150 of the God-called and God-led employees were forced into retirement There were no substantive explanations or discernible reasons. They were the leaders of the publishing house—including department and division directors—who had served for years with distinction and honor. No charges of heresy or incompetency were leveled against any of them. They were simply employed when the former leadership was in office. Almost without exception each had followed the call of God when employed. Likewise, administrative officials in charge believed these employments were God's will. Another group of 40 to 50 individuals was given the choice of early retirement to "clean out the old leadership."

In two seminaries almost all of the faculty members were fired, encouraged to find other employment, or scorned into leaving their positions. They were given no reason, except in less than a half-dozen cases the charge of "insubordination" or the reason of change in personnel policies.

The very able and dedicated president of Southwestern Baptist Theological Seminary was summarily fired because the fundamentalist board said, "We have the votes, and we don't need a reason." The two leading journalists at Baptist Press were fired by the Executive Committee without formal charges, legal representation, or the right to a hearing.

Public excoriation of so-called moderates by successive SBC presidents in public forums has been a common occurrence. Cooperative Baptist Fellowship members, churches, and activities are roundly condemned as "skunks, barnacles and excess baggage."

Such unchristian actions towards God's servants without opportunities to be heard and without substantive allegations of wrongdoing are not Scriptural. In its beginning, the financial structure of the Cooperative Baptist Fellowship was organized partly to help fund various SBC causes and bypass others. Churches and individuals continued to support the seminaries and the mission boards of the SBC through the CBF. The Southern Baptist Convention voted to refuse all funds from the churches and individuals sent through the CBF since this was seen as "competition with the Cooperative Program."

Biblical orthodoxy aside, the fundamentalists' messages are clearly those of force, control, conformity, judgment, and exclusivism. These messages are not biblical and do not properly represent the purposes of God in Scripture.

The problems related to the alienation of the public from the causes of the religious right (and conservative Christians) were by no means limited to Baptists. The Christian Coalition and the Moral Majority had wielded a heavy hand in dealing with social, educational, and moral issues. Heavy hitters such as Paul Weyrich, James Dobson, Cal Thomas, and numerous others have publicly and privately supported these right-winged groups because they fought against abortion and homosexuality and for family values and particularly the Republican Party. The marriage of conservative religion and conservative politics produced a curious medley of condemnation of Democrats and commendation of Republicans during the impeachment trial of the President. Widespread criticism of this sometimes-unholy alliance made the conservatives take another look at their standing with the public. Overwhelmingly the public supported the acquittal of the president, not because he was innocent but because his sins were not viewed as grounds for impeachment and the consequent national crisis. This left the religious right in a vulnerable position. The public obviously did not approve of the conduct of the chief executive, but equally did not approve of what they saw as an attempted political assassination. Further, they saw politicians "play dirty pool" which did not fit their oft-repeated biblical references.

In those places where the religious right had taken control of local elections, particularly of the school boards, criticism escalated and grew louder. Where attempts were made to put creationism into school curricula as a substitute or parallel to evolutionary theory the voices of resentment by many liberal groups grew. As it became clear that the Republican Party sympathized with fundamentalist Christians, the opposition became deafening.

The defeat at the polls, the defeat of impeachment of the president, the failure of the National Republican Party to acquiesce to the demands of conservatives, the defeat of Bob Dole for President, and dozens of other such debacles along with rising opposition seemed to derail the right-wing parade.

Paul Weyrich, founder of the Heritage Foundation and head of Coalitions for America, declared, "politics itself had failed." He asserted that mainstream culture was so corrupt that conservatives needed to withdraw and find a better way to effect their goals than the current political process. His public renunciation of the political arena set off a firestorm of debate. Weyrich was joined by other conservative stalwarts including Rev. Ed Dobson and commentator Cal Thomas. Their new book *Blinded by Might* criticized the core ideas behind the Moral Majority and the Christian Coalition. They argued that American society should be improved by changing individuals, not politics, and that conservative Christians have been tainted by their involvement in politics. They insisted the down side of Moral Majority's political involvement was an unhealthy focus on media coverage and fundraising. They noted their regrets at mixing religion and politics.

The return fire was not long in coming. Larry Arnn of the Claremont Institute and Ed Feulner of the Heritage Foundation said in the *Los Angeles Times* on March 16, 1999 that Weyrich's "strategy will lead to disaster" and that conservatives "should not allow impatience for final victory to cloud their judgment."

The Family Research Council ran ads on 200 radio stations urging conservatives to call Congress and "voice your values so Congress will value your voice."

Gary Bauer, late of The Family Research Council and now a candidate for of the Republican nomination for the presidency, said dropping out of politics was "a silly idea." He has since dropped out of the race for president.

D. James Kennedy of Coral Ridge Ministries said at the Reclaiming America for Christ conference: "To those who say that the culture war is over, I say, 'we have not yet begun to fight!'"

Accusations and recriminations reverberated across the media and some participants seemed to live on talk-show television. Criticism of the religious right rose to crescendo pitch in many quarters. Increasingly, conservative Christianity became more entangled with political strategies. Christians who had little patience with a political approach to morality were tarred with the same brush as the political activists.

One net effect of these controversies was that non-Christians, along with many believers, were wondering, where is the biblical message and what is the church doing?

As noted in chapter 6 on Conservative Christians and the Religious Right, two widely diverse groups were being "bashed" because they claimed to be Christians.

The Religious Right had spent a decade bashing all who dared to disagree. Now the shoe was on the other foot. As the criticism grew, the leaders of the Right complained that they were being unfairly attacked and shut out of the loop. Richard Land of the Ethics Commission of the SBC in his report to the convention said:

We live in a time of unprecedented moral and spiritual crisis in our nation. And in the very time when our nation most needs to hear a sure and certain word from God through his people, those in the media and those in the press and those in society who oppose us are doing their very best to oppress us.

Land was not invited by CNN to participate in a program on Southern Baptists. He accused CNN of slanting the news, as typical by their having a selection of guests that excludes people like him. Numerous similar attacks on the media have announced to the nation that the Religious Right is falling on harder times.

Make no mistake the Religious Right is by no means dead. New efforts are certain. The coalitions may divide or change names, but they are alive if not well.

Tragically, conservative Christians who do not subscribe to the political methodology to bring moral and ethical change have been classified with the politicians. As a result their message of reconciliation and love has been covered with political diatribes.

In this case, is the perception of the public of conservative Christianity the reality? Does the biblical message condemn, excoriate, and denigrate those who fall into wrongdoing? Is there no hope for the wayward? Is it sin or sins that alienate people from God? What has been God's message to the wayward from the beginning of revelation?

It is not "we have the votes!"

What is the Bible message to all of us who have "missed the mark"?

## The Bible or Politics

The message of Scripture is what it has always been. Untarnished with the hunger and search for power and control it is a message of the love of God for wayward man: "For God so loved the world that he gave his only son that whosoever believes in him should not perish but have everlasting life" (John 3:16).

> Jesus was thrust before Pilate, who asked him: 'Are you king of the Jews?' Jesus answered: 'My kingdom (kingship, royal power) belongs not to this world. If my kingdom were of this world, My followers would have been fighting to keep Me from being handed over to the Jews. But as it is, My kingdom [is not from this world] has no such origin or source...Certainly I am a king! This is why I was born, and for this I have come into the world to bear witness to the Truth. Everyone who is of the truth (who is a friend

of the truth, who belongs to the truth) hears and listens to my voice.' (John 18:36,37 Amplified NT)

When Jesus was asked about the obligations to governmental tax authority he said: "Render to Caesar the things that are Caesar's and to God the things that are God's" (Matthew 22:21).

When Jesus was asked what is the greatest commandment, he replied: "'Love the Lord your God with all your heart and with all your soul and with all your mind....The second is like it: Love your neighbor as yourself. All the Law and Prophets hang on these two commandments'" (Matthew 22:37,39,40 NIV).

The proof of the spiritual pudding: "We know that we have passed from death to life, because we love our brothers....This is how we know what love is: Jesus has laid down his life for us. And we ought to lay down our lives for our brothers" (1 John 3:14, 16).

"If you keep my commandments—if you continue to obey my instructions—you will abide in my love and live on in it; just as I have obeyed my Father's commandments and live on in his love" (John 15: 10 ANT).

When the disciples asked him who is the greatest in the kingdom of heaven, "He called a little child and had him stand among them. And he said: 'I tell you the truth, unless you change and become like little children, you will never enter the kingdom of heaven. Therefore, whoever humbles himself like this child is the greatest in the kingdom of heaven'" (Matthew 18:1-4 NIV).

On the important things in this life, Jesus said: "But seek you first the kingdom of God and his righteousness and all these things will be given to you as well (food, clothing and shelter) (Matthew 6:33).

"This is my commandment, that you love one another [just] as I have loved you." (John 15:12 ANT).

Is the message of the Religious Right political or Christian?

CHAPTER THIRTEEN

# WHY I AM A BAPTIST

### JAMES M. DUNN

Miz Lillian, President Carter's mother, grudgingly but cordially met a reporter at the door of her Plains, Georgia home. Jimmy was running for President, telling Americans, "I'll never lie to you."

The reporter, some sort of Yankee, tested the very senior sister Carter's patience. "Hasn't Jimmy Carter ever lied?" he asked.

" Oh, maybe, little white lies," mother Carter responded.

"What is a white lie?" he pushed.

" Oh, you know," she said, "like the one I told when I greeted you just now: 'It's so good to see you.'"

I was "brung up" with that standard for honesty. In our home a smile was sincere, a scowl was a scold, a compliment was a gracious gift.

Admonitions, which I am sure with Dr. Spock were far too frequent, and every single rebuff were honest attempts to help my sister Ann and me learn to make good choices on our own. We understood that, even then. Hard-core honesty laved with love left no doubt in our minds about where our parents stood or who they were or that we were loved.

To this good day I have trouble saying "it's so good to see you" when it is not. Small talk with mean-spirited people is difficult. I've thought a lot about that.

Oh, I know it was indeed a certain lack of socialization on the part of my parents, both children of sharecroppers. But it was much more than slim sophistication. Mother and Daddy had no patience with pretension. They could not stand people "putting on."

The other side of that coin of tough truthfulness, lived as well as said, was immense respect for every last person with whom they came in contact. They "loved folks just because they are folks," as T. B. Maston often said.

In retrospect, I've finally seen it. There is a two-sidedness to high expectation for candid, apparent, what-you-see-is-what-you-get personality on one hand and remarkable respect for every individual on the other. If people are what they present themselves to be, what more can one ask?

My parents came by these virtues honestly. Their little frame Baptist church at Cottonwood, Kaufman County was the locus of a fellowship that was formative. They took Scripture seriously; boy, did they! Spiritual formation suffused every ordinary chore. Hymn singing accompanied daily duties.

They had a primal insight into every human being as one made in God's image and one for whom Christ died. That permanent perspective installed infinite respect for persons.

That understanding of humanity included the view that one makes his own choices and lives with them. We are becoming more like ourselves every day by the slow stain of choice.

Whatever else the doctrine of *imago dei* involves, it means that we can respond to God. And much of our troubles and pain we bring upon ourselves. On the other hand, "you can do whatever you set your mind to." "Not failure, but low aim is crime." Everyone is able to respond, response able, responsible and free.

This is not a nuanced theology but one durable and deep, that elemental understanding which was ours for the acceptance of one's own personhood. We knew in our innards that all persons were valuable and fallible and free.

Hard honesty kept me from "going down the aisle" at church until I knew I meant it. Our church crept as close to compulsion as it could. The pastor fostered what we later came to call "trap services." Some of the preachers would literally try to scare the hell out of us. I resisted. I knew I was responsible for my own decision. When a kinder, gentler pastor came, I accepted Christ.

All that may sound unconnected to "Why I Am a Baptist." It's not.

Before falling into the clutches of manipulative Baptist evangelists, our family went to East Broadway Presbyterian in Fort Worth. It was wonderful. Lots of Bible. Pastors who qualified every pontification with "as I understand it" or "my own belief is." I can still smell the flour-and-water paste we made in Vacation Bible School and remember holding high my first pocket watch to signal the preacher I'd had enough sermon.

Our best neighbors were Campbellites (Church of Christ). So my child-hood was about as ecumenical as one could expect on the south side of Fort Worth.

Then, years later when college came, I had a heavy dose of Methodism at Texas Wesleyan College. It was the right school for me: small enough to know everyone, caring professors, and a healthy atmosphere of experienced religion.

Along through these experiences my religion was forming what I later learned to call theology. Some of the elemental components were:

- Respect for every person who like every pot sits on his or her own bottom, responsible and free,
- A presupposition that even God will not violate that faculty given every human to decide for himself,
- A belief that God, taking on flesh and blood and temptations like mine, in the human and divine Jesus, cared for me personally and for every other human being on the face of the earth: "God so loved the world...."
- A conscientious objection to running roughly over the freedom of any mortal, because they are all shaped like God and dignified to great worth because Jesus took on flesh like ours, for our sake.

When Ralph Phelps, an ethics professor at Southwestern Baptist Theological Seminary, applied the Gospel to race relations, he made me mad. However, because of my own upbringing, I saw that he was right.

When Stewart Newman, a philosophy professor, taught one of those tire-some 5-night-2-hours-every night-study courses on what Baptists believe, it rang true. He introduced me to soul freedom, religious liberty, and their corollary, the separation of church and state.

When, years later, I was exposed to Senator Ralph Yarborough's political populism and passion for working people, I understood. He, by his own clear testimony, got his political philosophy right out of his Baptist beliefs.

When John Kenneth Galbraith told David Frost that his "economics for everyman" probably came from teaching at his Baptist mother's knee about the freedom and dignity of persons deemed by God to be worth the blood of Christ, I identified with him.

It was *not trickle-down theology* from the top but *bubble-up belief* born of experience that exposed me to Baptists. As Grady Cothen puts it, the idea of "transactions with God on our own" was the norm, the self-evident standard for religious experience.

How could anyone possibly believe anything else? Unless religion is free, voluntary, personal, intimate, and inward, it is not worth anything anyway.

No. It is worse than worthless, because if it's second-hand, it may well keep one from ever experiencing the real thing: a vital, visceral, life-changing faith.

Our religion is more a matter of relationships, human and divine, than rational exercise and our theology, rightly "incarnational," is essentially a relationship with Jesus Christ. Theology, then, interprets religion, rather than religion merely expressing theology. Some of us identify with E. Y. Mullins' approach to our faith. In *The Christian Religion in Its Doctrinal Expression*, he had no patience with theology as a "system of philosophy" or "abstract intellectualism."

Absolutely no coercion can exist ever at all in matters of faith. The coercive state has no business messing with religion. When government touches religion, it always has the touch of mud. *When anyone's religious freedom is denied, everyone's religious freedom is endangered.*

On the thinking level, then, my sticking with Baptists is related to the experiential emphasis. The "I" at the center of our being even Almighty God will not trample. George W. Truett spoke to this Baptist doggedness in his famous sermon on the steps of the United States Capitol. "The right to private judgment is the crown jewel of humanity and for any person or institution to come between God and the soul is a blasphemous impertinence and a defamation of the crown rights of the Son of God."

So *experience* not *expectations*, even expectations of family or church, makes for authentic Christian faith.

Then *personal* allegiance to a living Lord, not *propositions,* mark genuine Baptist testimony. A fundamentalist leader of the Southern Baptist departure from baptistness shared his personal views at a meeting in Nashville. He said, "I learned when I was at Princeton that I cannot believe anything that I cannot understand." Poor little fellow. Where is faith?

C. S. Lewis said "If one can believe only what he can understand he can write his creed on a postage stamp." We have no binding creed but a freedom that encourages—no, *mandates* personal interpretation of Scripture. Our confession of faith is the most ancient, the most accessible, the most biblical, the most universal, and the most pregnant with ethical and moral meaning of any Christian confession of faith. It is simply, "Jesus Christ is Lord."

If we have anything remotely resembling a creed it is the Baptist oral tradition that insists, *"Ain't nobody but Jesus going to tell me what to believe."*

Finally, it is a *relationship* to Jesus Christ, not a *rational scheme* that puts one right with God. You may call it too subjective. You may call it gnostic. Say that it is cowboy Christianity with "every man's hat his church." Baptists have historically held the objective-subjective balance between *sola scriptura* and *sola fide*. No list of laws, no articles of assent, no head-trip makes one righteous. Rather, repentance and faith are steps of Grace.

Bernard Ramm in a wonderful little book, *The Pattern of Authority*, suggests that Baptist Christians find the ultimate authority in the living Lord, Jesus Christ as revealed in Scripture, or the Scripture as it becomes the Living Word through the work of Jesus Christ in our lives. Doesn't matter which way you say it, does it?

Conformity, convention, coercion, consensus, cannot redeem. *In fact, "free" and "faithful" are the hallmarks of real Baptists.*

On a feeling level, I've found the faith mediated to me by Baptists worthy. Who hasn't sung, "Tempted and tried we're oft made to wonder, why it should be thus all the day long." Even if you do not know the song, you have felt the feeling. In 1974, invasive melanoma planted me in the Stehlin Research Institute for a month and had me planning my funeral. My faith was tested. I came to know "the peace that passes understanding."

When the experiences of life shake you by the nape of the neck like a mother cat claims back a kitten, faith is tested. When everything you believe is challenged, faith is tested. The vitality of a baptist-kind of religious experience has served me well. My life's experiences are not smaltzy sentimentalities that drip like a bottle of thick, gooey syrup or ooze like a festering sore. My experiences are not fake, Pollyanna happy faces. Neither are they ice-cold, steely stoicism. My life is a *faithing* of my way forward being sustained in the Baptist fellowship.

Plenty of folks labeled "Baptists" embarrass me. Television entrepreneurs, sleazy politicians, cocksure, arrogant fundamentalists. But Baptists on our good days, when we are living up to our profession of faith, are a breed with whom I am proud to claim kinship.

We find evangelism, ministry, and mission fueled by love. We find passion for peace and justice and meeting human need. We find the pursuit of truth and learning, art and free expression. We find personal spiritual growth, maturity, and Christian insight. Much of what moderns search for they can find if they encounter a better bunch of Baptists. Such families of faith do exist.

However, in Washington when I tell someone "Yes, I'm a Baptist and I work for Baptists," his or her response often drips with snide. I hurriedly say, "But I'm a Bill Moyers, Jimmy Carter, Barbara Jordan kind of Baptist."

How about you?

CHAPTER FOURTEEN

# WHY I AM STILL A BAPTIST

GRADY C. COTHEN

*Humankind*
*Man was created by the special act of God, in His own image, and is the*
*crowning work of His creation. In the beginning, man was innocent of*
*sin and was endowed by his Creator with freedom of choice. By his free*
*choice, man sinned against God and brought sin into the human race....*
*Only the grace of God can bring man into His holy fellowship and enable*
*man to fulfill the creative purpose of God. The sacredness of human per-*
*sonality is evident in that God created man in His own image, and in*
*that Christ died for man; therefore every man possesses dignity and is*
*worthy of respect and Christian love.*

*The Baptist Faith and Message, 1963*

"...Grace...that not of yourselves...a gift from God." Ephesians 2:8

If one could be born a Baptist, I was. My father was a small-town and
country preacher. He was thoroughly Baptist. How he ever learned what he
knew about being a Baptist with his limited education is beyond me. But he
was a Baptist in the best sense of the word.

I was reared in the Southern Baptist way of doing things. Looking back,
it was rather simple, encompassing, organized, and consistent. It was natural
and expected to attend church twice on Sundays and always on Wednesday
night. Of course, there was Sunday school, with Scripture at the center of the
session after the usual palaver about the events of the week. On Sunday

evening before the worship service, there was BYPU. The letters meant Baptist Young Peoples Union. It became Baptist Training Union and Discipleship. In those days the program was divided into "parts" given by the participants. The leader insisted that the parts be given without reading from the book. Sometimes they were.

At least once a month on Wednesdays the Sunbeams, the Royal Ambassadors, and the Girls' Auxiliary met. These were organizations designed to teach boys and girls of different ages the basics of missions education.

We had Sword Drills, which were designed to familiarize us with the Bible and its different books and give us the ability to find a passage quickly. Competition was frequently keen and sometimes became the emphasis.

The Royal Ambassador organization sponsored a speakers program that climaxed in a statewide competition among boys of similar ages. I entered, won in the county, and lost miserably in the state competition. It was at this point, however, that I began to feel some small lessening of my terror of public speaking.

The Sunday school experience was graded on a point record system. The grading system required reports on the Bible given on time, lessons studied, offering given, worship attended, and some others. Tithing was frequently taught and practiced by a remarkable number of loyal, faithful Baptists.

Scholars, professors, and other learned critics have roundly criticized this approach. Some label it as juvenile, elementary, immature, and inadequate to produce scholarly Bible study. While some points are correct, this approach was infinitely superior to what has followed.

Despite its shortcomings there were eternal consequences. We were familiar with the Bible. We knew about the grace of God for sinners. We knew we were sinners. The system was designed to lead individuals to salvation through Jesus Christ. It helped one develop the habit of reading the Bible regularly and despite human frailty one remembered a great deal of it. The confrontation of responsibility for self and to a degree for others was a constant. We gained a minimal knowledge of mission personnel, activities, and responsibility for them. We learned the organizations and functions of Baptist life and something about those who led these activities.

This Baptist upbringing that went on in the 1920s, 1930s, and to a lesser degree in the 1940s and 1950s was sprinkled with "hell-fire" preaching, vigorous congregational singing, revival meetings that sometimes lasted two weeks, and some generous guilt trips. After all these years and the state of the culture today, a little Baptist guilt would be very healthy.

There were generous doses of scripture memorization along the way. In our home around the supper table each of the four boys and our parents quoted a scripture passage before the prayer of thanksgiving. If a boy quoted the same passage more than twice in succession, he learned another before eating. In seminary the evangelism professor had us memorize a scripture passage each day. I discovered to my amazement that I already knew most of them.

As you would suppose, at home we were taught that "Each of us shall give an account of himself to God' (Romans 14:12) Scripture was buttressed with such Mississippi wisdom as "Every tub must sit on its own bottom." "You made your bed now sleep in it." Or, "You have to paddle your own canoe." In retrospect, several aspects of this rigorous training stand out after more than a half-century. "Responsibility" looms large. "Grace" is written on the heart from the unerasable Book and the needs of human frailty. "The will of God" posted many crossroads with "This is the way, walk ye in it." The Bible was the authority and "the Bible said it, I believe it, and that settles it."

The years have raised many questions. The skeptics and critics have quizzed the old ways. What passes for modern wisdom belittles much from those sometimes laborious exercises and long-gone years.

From it all and a Christian family, I came out a Baptist. A look back assures me still that AUTHORITY FOR A BAPTIST IS THE BIBLE! There were no official interpretations. No other Baptist body told our little churches what they must believe or who they may call as pastor or what they must give to what or how much. No one gave us a required list of "parameters" circumscribing Scripture.

Scripture was the sole rule of faith and practice. The reason it was so is that the Bible is the inspired Word of God. As a result, we were dependent on God's grace and forgiveness. The church and its fellowship were more important than anything else going on in town. The family was first after God and received first attention.

The church was not viewed as a museum for the display of perfect saints, but as a hospital for limping souls. It was theoretically democratic in its local manifestation. If push came to shove, it was in fact. The church was independent and autonomous. No one outside the local fellowship was entitled to participate in its decisions or dictate its activities. Its cooperation with fellow believers was voluntary and subject to review.

Yet, the churches usually chose to enlarge their ministries by establishing relationships with others of "like faith and order." The local association of churches was a convenient way of relating to others, carrying on mission work, opposing the forces of alcohol, gambling, or other causes. The state convention supported colleges, orphanages, starting new churches, retirement plans for pastors, and other projects. The national body supported the seminaries and mission enterprises over the world. The local church expanded its ministry through cooperation with others of a like mind.

When the time came, the rubber hit the road and the water hit the wheel and the work was done in the local church. It provided worship, ministry, witness, Christian education, spiritual development, nurture, and fellowship. There was a strong emphasis on regenerate church membership, believer's baptism, and the Lordship of Christ. Many of the fracases the churches got into revolved around these important issues.

The relationships in the local body enhanced its ability to minister to the many needs demanding the churches' attention. Through their cooperative ministry, the churches provided for my education. Mississippi College in those days was small and poor. However, it had an outstanding faculty. They knew us all by first names and something about most of our backgrounds and were really interested in seeing to it that we were exposed to an education. They understood that there was no necessary correlation between a degree and an education.

Our churches felt the necessity for a trained ministry. I wanted to go to Southwestern Seminary since most of my class was going to Southern. I did not have money enough to get there. I settled for New Orleans Seminary, then called the Baptist Bible Institute. It was even smaller and poorer than the college but also had a faculty that would grace even the more prestigious schools of today.

Somehow, the denomination saw no necessity for constant interference with or prompting or controlling of all of these activities. These entities were agencies of the churches. They were not considered to be extensions of some denominational power brokers. The denomination in those years was interested in "Baptistness."

By this time in my own experiences, I had become a Baptist by conviction as well as by family ties. Some things had become clear:

• All this Baptist business was voluntary.
• Even at the seminary I was free to be or not to be.
• I had the nurture and the wisdom of the Body of Christ available to me.
• I was free to participate, cooperate, and support or not support according to the dictates of my conscience.
• Responsibility loomed large and would not go away.

• My accountability was primarily to God and went on to the church, family, and the larger family of God. The accountability to God was not a matter for the judgment of others, while relationships to others was also a matter of conscience but for which I was accountable to God.

One of the great blessings of life has been coming to know the larger family of God spread across the world. Once in Berlin, just inside the wall, I preached to a German congregation. When it was over one saint said to me: "I see you know the same Christ we know." At the end of World War II, first off the ship with occupation troops, I met a Japanese man. "American?" "Yes, I am an American." "Christian?" "Yes I am a Christian." "Me too!" he said. And the war was over.

As I went along the usual course followed by my generation of young men, some things became clearer. Spiritually I was following the train of Thomas Helwys, Roger Williams, John Leland, E. Y. Mullins, and George Truett. Here were forbears who believed in a free conscience constricted only by the Bible. They had paid a great price—Helwys with his life—for the principles of free exercise of religion.

Government had no place in religious exercise and religion had no control of the functions of government. Christians had responsibility for being good citizens and government provided for the freedom to practice citizenship.

There was no official interpretation of Scripture and no doctrinal straight jacket to constrict it. As I read and studied Scripture I came to believe the Holy Spirit helped me to understand its message. Within my limits, there was something in the Book for me and God often met me there. I was, even with my limitations, able to meet and transact business with God for myself.

Soul Competence.

This privilege was not unique to me. It was—and is—available to everyone. I had no corner on truth and sometimes I mistook what God was saying to me. In time, He would try to get my head straight.

The matters of church and state, so confused in American society today, at the time seemed to be simple. Compulsory religious practices, whether implemented by ecclesiastical or governmental forces, violated God's relationship with believers. If another made—or makes—one's religious decisions, they cannot be valid religious transactions. Force or undue influence in religion negates a proper relationship to God. If one is dependent on another for decision, interpretation, access, or religious privilege, there is no soul competence or independence or at least responsibility. In such circumstance, priesthood is sacrificed and personal growth is stunted.

It was and is clear that I am to be a responsible Christian citizen. It is important to be a wholesome Christian influence in all relationships. However, that does not come by intimidation or force. Relationships between schools and churches in those days were much simpler in our part of the country. Christians were overwhelmingly in the majority and cooperation (and competition) was a part of our lives. For example, one year the school met in the Methodist church—no charge—while a building was being replaced. The one Catholic family in town did not object, and if anyone did we were not aware of it.

In my study of other religious bodies, the problematic matter of governance of the church was disturbing. The freedom of the local body of believers in some cases was an illusion. In other cases, the hierarchy made religious decisions and handed them down to the individual or church, thus removing responsibility from the individual. In other cases, the control of government over the activities of the church was clearly invasive of faith expression and responsibility to God. So, in 1999 even the English are arguing over disestablishing the Anglican Church.

During the Second World War, I served as a Navy chaplain. One of my concerns during that hectic time was whether the government that paid me would try to dictate my religious activity. It did not. I was under the command structure of the military but not one time did any superior attempt to dictate my religious conduct. There were other chaplains of many religious stripes and they had the same duties and opportunities to witness to their faith as I did.

It was here that I learned first hand how different my faith was from many others. They had all the rights and responsibilities I had. In the civilian setting after the war others did not support my faith by way of tax money, nor did I support their faith. This was right and proper and we all prospered according to God's good blessings.

I came to believe—and still do—that I had no noose of presuppositions of others about my religious neck. No one could pressure or coerce my religious faith and practice. Religious freedom and free exercise of religion were my inheritance.

Again, I was responsible for my actions and myself. First to God, then the church of my choosing, my family, and the larger community of believers. My faith is not to be restricted by some one's words about faith and/or the Bible.

But I am surrounded, trapped, restricted, hemmed in, directed, limited, confronted and endlessly blessed by the Bible.

There is here nothing of the isolationism of the often-mentioned personalism or individualism or lone-wolfism charged by fundamentalists. Here is a relationship to God, for which I am responsible. Here is a relationship to fellow believers. Here is responsibility for what I am and what I do for God and the church. Here is no room for others to dictate what I am to believe or give orders as to my religious duties.

Nor am I holy or wise enough to give religious orders to others. If I can help with their cooperation and consent, then I must. I can nurture, teach, serve, and love but I must not intrude.

These things are here repeated since they have so little currency with many. My confession:

A competent but imperfect soul before a Holy God.

As He is revealed in Scripture.

Responsible.


These are the things I was taught that make an authentic Baptist. I am sure that I do not fit the prescription of some, but I think I am a traditional and biblical Baptist.